JACKED PHP

Create Powerful Applications With Open Swoole

by Savio Resende

a php[architect] guide

Jacked PHP
Create Powerful Applications With Open Swoole

php[architect] edition published: TBD

Print ISBN:	978-1-940111-99-5
PDF ISBN:	978-1-957147-05-5
ePub ISBN:	978-1-957147-06-2

Produced & Printed in the United States

Disclaimer

Written by
Savio Resende

Managing Editor
John Congdon

Layout
John Congdon

Published by
PHP Architect, LLC.
13366 Samantha Ave
San Diego, CA 92129 USA

406-PHP-ARCH (406-747-2724)
info@phparch.com
www.phparch.com

Table of Contents

Dedication

To my beloved wife and daughter, whose love, patience and understanding have been my sanctuary, my inspiration and strength. You have been my rock, my joy, and my inspiration every step of the way. My parents, whose unwavering support and endless love have been my guiding stars. Your sacrifices, encouragement, and belief in me have been the foundation upon which I have built my dreams.

This book is a testament to all the wonderful people who have walked this path with me. Thank you for being part of my story.

– *Sávio Resende*

About The Author

Sávio Resende has worked in Software Engineering for more than 19 years. He's worked for many companies in the public and private sectors, having had the opportunity to work for Brazil's Federal Government. Between the private sector's projects, he worked in projects that served MIT, London's Metropolitan Archives, Costco Hearing Aid Centre, and more…

Sávio is a Co-Author with Peter MacIntyre on the book *WordPress Development in Depth* published by phparch.com[1], Co-Organizer of some PHP Meetups in the past and gives presentations on programming related subjects. Sávio is brazilian-canadian and now lives in Texas, with his family.

[1] https://www.phparch.com/

Foreword

I first met Savio while I was attending a WordPress conference in Seattle Washington a few years ago (pre-pandemic). We connected with each other over PHP and web development ideas that went much deeper than just surface level WordPress issues.

WordPress plugin and theme development were just the beginning. After that conference we stayed in touch and a few months later I had a technical book writing project (WordPress Development in Depth - PHP Architect) that I wanted him to consider co-authoring with me. He was sharp and super-keen when I first met him at the conference and he was equally as sharp and keen to work on a technical writing project with me. His ability to explain complex topics in simple and easy to understand terms is what every wrangler of technology subject matter should possess.

Over the years that followed our first meeting we have worked together on a few PHP projects as well as some other technical writing projects. Savio has proven to be both a great communicator and technical writer at every turn. I am also glad to count him among my friends in the world of technology.

If you want to get in depth knowledge as well as neat tips and tricks on Swoole then this is the place to start. Savio will guide you safely from start to finish in clear and straightforward language. As well, he will help you side-step the pitfalls and "gotchas" you may encounter along the way.

Peter MacIntyre, PEI, Canada

Chapter

1

PHP and the new web challenges

The new technologies out there accomplished great things. Products like Netflix, Google Docs, and AWS… are pushing the market forward, offering new solutions and giving a new understanding of what's possible. Because of this constant movement towards more complex, faster, available, and maintainable web apps, old monoliths are losing space. The community has been electing this or that tool occasionally to build with these non-functional requirements (e.g., performance, scalability, etc.). In the PHP world, we have seen a lot of frameworks and tools that aim to help developers build better products. Laravel, Symfony, and Zend are some of the most popular frameworks, and they are great. They offer a lot of tools to help developers build better products. But, we need to look further when we talk about performance, scalability, and maintainability. That's where OpenSwoole comes in.

This book aims to offer the developer tools to build better products. Since being faster and scalable is in high demand, looking for tools to support that becomes essential. With that in mind, we have a set of tools within the OpenSwoole framework that we will go over that can help you achieve these goals. We built a great set of tools with the usual PHP, from controlling Linux processes to listening to TCP connections to serve websites with data retrieved from multiple sources. We are not talking about an extensive set of things PHP could not do; we are talking about a new way of working with PHP with a framework that makes it more accessible and faster.

In this book, we will first review OpenSwoole, what it is, what is achievable, and what differs from the standard PHP. After that, we will visit topics for your development environment, debugging tools/strategies, and dockerization (or containerization). Once you are all set, we will see several use cases. Within those cases, we will see HTTP web servers, WebSockets and Real-time technology, Coroutines and Multitasking, and Finally, we will go over Process Management; we will use the opportunity to use a large group of the technologies we reviewed through the chapters so you see how they fit together.

I hope you enjoy this book and that it helps you to build better products. Also, to get through some complex topics with the examples presented here. If you have any questions, please feel free to contact me. I will be happy to help you.

Chapter 2

PHP OpenSwoole

According to OpenSwoole's website, OpenSwoole is a "(…) high-performance, scalable, concurrent TCP, UDP, Unix Socket, HTTP, WebSocket services with PHP and easy to use coroutine, fibers API." (Reference: https://openswoole.com). All of that means that you will be able to (1) stream, (2) work with realtime apps, (3) build different components that collaborate with a "pass the baton strategy" (while one is working on something, the other can start doing something else while there is no return form the first). All of this is in the context of functionalities that are easier to do with OpenSwoole but achievable without.

There are many benefits when using PHP OpenSwoole. Benefits such as performance and simplified asynchronous programming. With that in hand, we have a solution that "… enhances the efficiency of your PHP applications and brings you out of the traditional stateless model, enabling you to focus on the development of innovative products at a large scale, bringing event loops and asynchronous programming to the PHP language." (https://openswoole.com/docs)

PHP Context

At its core, PHP is a set of extensions bundled together. Each extension is a C package built for specific purposes, enhancing PHP's capabilities and allowing it to perform a wide range of functions. These extensions are a testament to PHP's modular architecture, which enables developers to include only the necessary functionalities for their projects, thereby optimizing performance and reducing overhead.

The versatility of PHP extensions means that the language can accomplish almost anything achievable with C, the foundational language for these extensions. PHP's ability to interface directly with C libraries allows for the creation of powerful and efficient web applications. This capability extends PHP's reach beyond simple web page generation to include tasks such as image processing, database interaction, cryptography, and more.

One of the primary advantages of PHP is its ease of use. PHP syntax is straightforward and easy to learn, especially for those familiar with other C-like languages. This simplicity makes PHP an excellent choice for beginners while still offering advanced features for experienced developers. PHP code can be embedded directly into HTML, making it an ideal language for developing dynamic web pages.

Unlike Node.js, which relies on JavaScript's event-driven, non-blocking I/O model, OpenSwoole brings similar capabilities to PHP, but with the added advantage of coroutines. Coroutines allow for more granular control over concurrency, reducing overhead and improving performance. This makes PHP with OpenSwoole highly competitive for building high-concurrency applications, such as real-time chat systems, games, and APIs, often outperforming Node.js in benchmarks.

Leveraging OpenSwoole, PHP significantly enhances its capabilities, making it a powerful choice for modern web development. OpenSwoole integrates seamlessly with popular frameworks like Laravel, Symfony, and CodeIgniter, which already provide developers with structured, reusable code and promote best practices such as the MVC (Model-View-Controller) architecture. This architecture separates business logic from presentation logic, ensuring cleaner and more maintainable code.

OpenSwoole's advanced features, such as asynchronous programming and built-in web server capabilities, complement these frameworks by providing a high-performance environment for PHP applications. This combination allows developers to build scalable and efficient applications with ease. Moreover, these frameworks offer built-in tools for common tasks like authentication, routing, and form validation, which, when paired with OpenSwoole's performance enhancements, enable developers to focus on creating unique features and delivering a superior user experience.

PHP OpenSwoole Extension

Now that we have this brief explanation of PHP's context, it is crucial to understand how OpenSwoole enhances PHP's capabilities. As a powerful PHP extension, OpenSwoole brings a suite of advanced features to the language, all accessible through a straightforward interface.

Firstly, OpenSwoole introduces asynchronous programming to PHP, allowing developers to write non-blocking code that can handle multiple tasks simultaneously without waiting for each task to complete before moving on to the next. This is particularly beneficial for I/O-bound operations such as database queries, file handling, and network requests, significantly improving the efficiency and responsiveness of applications.

Secondly, OpenSwoole enables PHP to serve as its own web server. This built-in web server capability eliminates the need for traditional web servers like Apache or Nginx, streamlining the deployment process and reducing overhead. With OpenSwoole, PHP can handle HTTP requests directly, providing faster request handling and improved performance.

Lastly, OpenSwoole offers robust process management features. It allows developers to create and manage multiple processes and threads within a PHP application, facilitating the development of highly scalable and concurrent applications. This includes features such as process pools, task workers, and timers, which help manage complex workflows and background tasks efficiently.

By incorporating these advanced features, OpenSwoole transforms PHP into a more powerful and versatile tool, capable of competing with other high-performance frameworks and languages. This extension leverages PHP's existing strengths while addressing its traditional limitations, making it an ideal choice for modern, high-demand web applications.

Asynchronous programming

Asynchronous programming is a powerful technique that allows applications to handle multiple tasks concurrently, without waiting for each task to complete before starting the next one. In PHP, achieving asynchronous behavior traditionally required complex configurations and integrating various technology stacks. These setups, while effective, often involved a steep learning curve and introduced limitations in terms of scalability and ease of maintenance. Over time, certain methods and technologies became standard practice, but these standards were not always user-friendly or straightforward to implement.

OpenSwoole provides a more intuitive and streamlined approach to writing asynchronous code, allowing developers to reap the benefits of concurrent processing without the typical overhead associated with traditional methods. With OpenSwoole, developers can write non-blocking code that handles multiple tasks simultaneously, significantly improving the efficiency and performance of their applications.

One of the primary advantages of OpenSwoole is its intuitive interface. The framework abstracts much of the complexity involved in asynchronous programming, offering developers a set of easy-to-use tools and functions to manage concurrency. This predictability and simplicity make it accessible to both novice and experienced developers, reducing the barrier to entry and accelerating the development process.

PHP application using OpenSwoole can handle multiple database queries in parallel, reducing the overall execution time and improving user experience. Similarly, network requests can be processed concurrently, allowing the application to serve more users simultaneously without a significant performance hit. These benefits are particularly valuable for high-demand applications that require fast response times and efficient resource utilization.

The WebServer independency

Having a dependency on a web server is another common aspect of PHP. Only recently, some initiatives offered the possibility of PHP serving production-ready servers by itself. The familiar places for a web server selection were Apache[1] [2] and NGINX[3] [4] (this last one still being important in some communities using OpenSwoole).

It was an exciting technology breakthrough when NodeJS[5] [6] came out with the strategy of web servers creation with a few lines of JavaScript code, and it would be a matter of time for some PHP technologies to do the same. Even though other programming languages did the same before, PHP and JavaScript became a massive fever in the last 20 years of the web, and, for PHP, an important factor is its low learning curve.

NodeJS and PHP servers are all based on Event Loops constructs and attach callbacks to specific events such as “start” or “request”. With that in hand, you can control the WebServer aspect of your application with PHP code instead of some Apache of NGINX configuration file with its not-trivial specifications that very often cost a lot of the development and

[1] *https://apache.org*
[2] *https://apache.org*
[3] *https://www.nginx.com*
[4] *https://www.nginx.com*
[5] *https://nodejs.org/*
[6] *https://nodejs.org/*

devOp's time. Now, on PHP Universe, we have options like PHP OpenSwoole, React PHP[7] [8] or AMP[9] [10]. All these options are functional and production ready. They, of course, face different challenges and circumstances based on the architectural decisions and the community around them that sometimes focus on other things. In this book, we will cover PHP OpenSwoole.

Performance

PHP is notably a fast programming language when it comes to performance. It is straightforward and efficient, making it a popular choice for web development. While we will discuss various performance optimization strategies in more detail later in this book, let's briefly cover what makes PHP OpenSwoole stand out among other PHP solutions.

PHP OpenSwoole significantly enhances performance by introducing asynchronous programming and coroutine-based concurrency to PHP. This advanced functionality allows PHP to handle multiple tasks simultaneously, dramatically improving efficiency and throughput. On benchmarks presented on OpenSwoole's website, we can see cases where the server reaches incredible numbers, such as 299,103.32 requests per second. This showcases OpenSwoole's superior performance and capacity to manage high-concurrency applications effectively.

> *Reference: https://web.archive.org/web/20230330141126/https://openswoole.com/benchmark (extracted from https://openswoole.com/benchmark)*

The Server Performance Aspect

The reason for such a performance increase involves several key aspects. Firstly, it is due to the way the PHP OpenSwoole framework operates. OpenSwoole creates multiple workers to handle parallel requests efficiently. In contrast, traditional setups rely on the web server layer to scale, which is less efficient than the PHP layer. Although additional extensions and specific strategies, such as the pthreads PECL extension for multithreading, can enhance performance, these solutions often require developers to manage a considerable extra overhead.

---

[7] https://reactphp.org
[8] https://reactphp.org
[9] https://amphp.org
[10] https://amphp.org

PHP OpenSwoole, on the other hand, natively supports scaling at the request level, significantly boosting development speed and efficiency. The framework's architecture involves a process manager overseeing blocking I/O calls and taking care of the details that might slow down your code that you lack control of (which is one of the reasons OpenSwoole is built as an extension). This management system allows the handling of concurrent tasks without requiring extensive manual configuration.

For a more detailed understanding of how PHP OpenSwoole achieves this, refer to Figure 1, which illustrates the relationship between workers, task workers, the process manager, reactors, and timers. For those interested in delving deeper into the technical specifics, I recommend consulting resources like Mastering Swoole PHP[11] or The Linux Programming Interface[12]. These books provide comprehensive insights into the framework's underlying mechanisms and advanced usage.

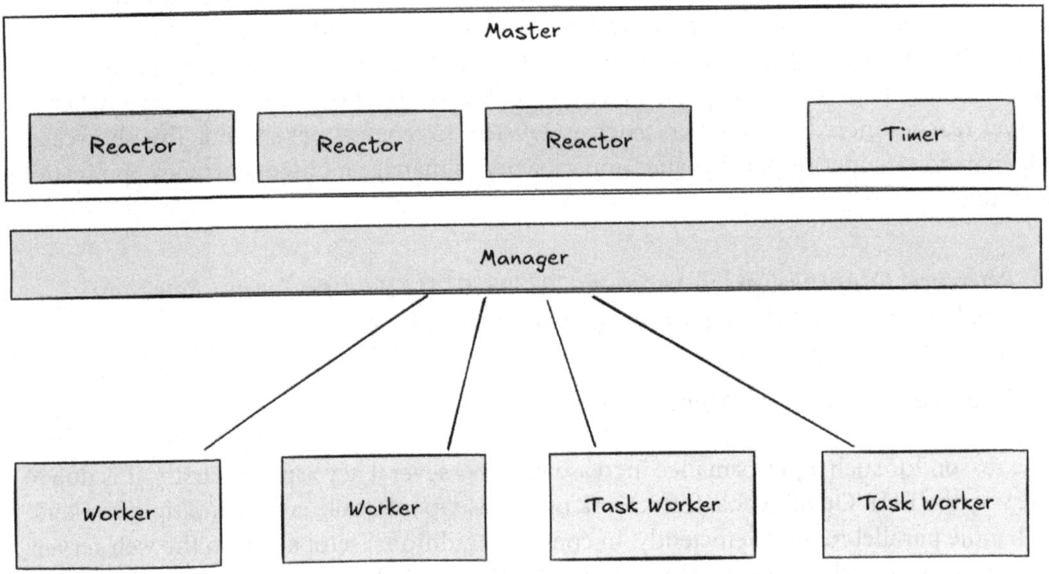

How Swoole Works. Reference: https://www.swoole.co.uk/how-it-works

[11] https://swoolebook.com/
[12] https://man7.org/tlpi/

The Memory Performance Aspect

Another game-changing aspect of PHP OpenSwoole is that it loads the source code into memory. This approach significantly alters the programming experience and requires developers to take extra steps to ensure the updated code runs correctly in the development environment. While we will touch on this topic later in this chapter, detailed discussions about development environment alternatives will be covered in Chapter 3.

Unlike PHP-FPM, which reloads and interprets the entire source code on every request, OpenSwoole keeps the code in memory, ready to handle subsequent requests instantly. This eliminates the overhead of repeatedly loading and interpreting scripts, thereby enhancing performance.

Furthermore, PHP OpenSwoole provides tools to manage memory between requests, allowing developers to share data and maintain the application state across requests. This shared memory capability extends to multiple clients, enabling more complex and efficient solutions. In contrast, achieving similar functionality with PHP-FPM typically involves storing data in a database or files, which introduces additional latency due to retrieval operations.

By keeping the code and shared data in memory, PHP OpenSwoole inherently operates faster and more efficiently. This memory-resident approach reduces the need for repeated I/O operations, making it an ideal choice for high-performance, real-time applications.

The PHP OpenSwoole Framework

The PHP OpenSwoole extension is a robust framework for working with coroutines and asynchronous programming. Its design facilitates a range of advanced tools and features, such as Coroutine Servers, MySQL drivers, and even a PCNTL substitute called Swoole Process. These tools and many others available within OpenSwoole significantly extend PHP's capabilities in modern development. OpenSwoole's Coroutines interface represents a significant advancement for the PHP ecosystem. They provide a new paradigm for asynchronous programming in PHP, allowing developers to write non-blocking code that can handle multiple tasks concurrently. Even though it is not the only alternative nowadays, it is a solid solution and a robust framework. We delve into Coroutines in Chapter 6.

One distinguishing feature of OpenSwoole is its use of PHP-CLI, which diverges from the traditional, stateless request-processing model commonly associated with PHP web programming. This shift lets developers exercise greater control over the application state and server processes. In that context, it is important to note one critical detail: while using

OpenSwoole features within a PHP-FPM environment is technically possible, doing so can lead to unpredictable results, as the system is optimized for PHP-CLI.

With PHP OpenSwoole, you can manage Unix processes directly, allowing you to start, terminate, and handle subprocesses as needed. Also, OpenSwoole excels in real-time programming, offering various server types that cater to different needs. This capability is one of the primary benefits of OpenSwoole, enabling the development of high-performance, real-time applications with ease.

By leveraging these advanced features, developers can create more efficient, scalable, and responsive applications, positioning PHP OpenSwoole as a significant enhancement to the PHP ecosystem.

Installing OpenSwoole

As an extension, PHP OpenSwoole is installable via PECL. You can install it by running the following command on your machine if you have PECL available:

```
pecl install openswoole
```

If you are using a Debian-based Linux distribution, you can use aptitude to install PHP OpenSwoole. First, add the necessary repositories, then install the PHP OpenSwoole package:

```
apt update
apt install -y software-properties-common && add-apt-repository ppa:ondrej/php -y
apt install -y software-properties-common && add-apt-repository ppa:openswoole/ppa -y

sudo apt-get -y install php8.2-openswoole
```

For a comprehensive guide, refer to the official documentation: OpenSwoole Installation Guide[13]. We will cover more strategies and details in Chapter 3. Note that the aptitude (and/or other package managers) might not have the latest version, so it is always recommended to use pecl.

[13] https://openswoole.com/docs/get-started/installation

Conclusion

In this chapter, we introduced PHP OpenSwoole, a powerful extension that enhances PHP's capabilities by introducing asynchronous programming, built-in web server functionality, and robust process management features. We discussed how OpenSwoole leverages PHP's existing strengths while addressing its traditional limitations, making it an ideal choice for modern web development.

Chapter 3

The Development Environment

Examples of this chapter: https://phpa.me/jacked-php-chapter-3

PHP OpenSwoole is a robust coroutine framework that operates as an extension to PHP rather than a traditional MVC (Model-View-Controller) framework. Unlike MVC frameworks that provide a structured approach to building typical websites, OpenSwoole offers tools to facilitate using async procedures in PHP applications. This distinction is crucial for understanding how OpenSwoole fundamentally alters certain base functionalities within the PHP environment, particularly in the context of web servers.

To fully grasp the capabilities and implications of PHP OpenSwoole, it is essential to delve into its core aspects and understand how it can be practically implemented. This book will provide numerous examples to help you navigate and use OpenSwoole. These examples are designed to be accessible, assuming you have a basic understanding of PHP programming—at the very least, the ability to write and run a simple "Hello World" script in a browser. If you are not yet comfortable with this level of PHP proficiency, we recommend you familiarize yourself with some introductory tutorials or foundational books on PHP programming before proceeding.

PHP OpenSwoole significantly enhances the PHP landscape by introducing a coroutine-based architecture, which can lead to more efficient and scalable applications. Coroutines in PHP allow for asynchronous programming, enabling the execution of multiple tasks simultaneously without blocking the main execution thread. This can result in improved performance and responsiveness, particularly for I/O-bound operations, such as database queries, file system interactions, and network requests. The tradeoff is complexity, which is why it is crucial to understand core concepts to know when unexpected behaviors happen.

The web server component of OpenSwoole is particularly noteworthy. Traditional PHP applications rely on external web servers like Apache or Nginx to handle HTTP requests. These web servers process requests by invoking the PHP interpreter, which can introduce latency and overhead. OpenSwoole, however, embeds a web server directly within the PHP application. This approach allows PHP scripts to handle HTTP requests natively, reducing latency and overhead and providing finer control over request handling and resource management.

By integrating the web server into the PHP runtime, OpenSwoole significantly simplifies the deployment process. Developers can deploy PHP applications as standalone services without additional web server configurations, eliminating an entire layer of complexity. This streamlining can result in a more efficient development workflow, as developers no longer need to manage separate web server setups or troubleshoot compatibility issues between the web server and PHP. Furthermore, the simplification extends to DevOps and infrastructure management. With one less layer to maintain, there is a reduction in operational overhead and the potential points of failure. This not only eases the burden on development teams but also enhances system reliability and reduces the costs associated with infrastructure management.

Moreover, OpenSwoole supports various advanced features that enhance its utility and flexibility. These features include task scheduling, which allows developers to offload intensive computations or background tasks to separate worker processes, and timer management, which facilitates the scheduling of periodic tasks. Additionally, OpenSwoole provides robust support for WebSockets, enabling the development of real-time applications such as chat systems, live notifications, and online gaming platforms.

Throughout this book, we will explore these features in detail, providing practical examples and guidance on how to leverage OpenSwoole to build high-performance, scalable PHP applications. We will cover topics such as setting up the OpenSwoole environment, creating and managing coroutines, handling HTTP requests and responses, working with WebSockets, and implementing task scheduling and timers.

Difference from PHP_FPM

Several key differences between PHP-FPM and OpenSwoole can significantly impact your development experience. This section will highlight the most crucial aspects to consider when transitioning from PHP-FPM to OpenSwoole.

Application in memory

The most significant difference lies in how each manages memory. In PHP-FPM, each incoming request is handled independently, with a new set of variables and context initialized from scratch. The only information shared between requests is session data or data persisted in filesystems or databases. For every request, PHP-FPM reloads the entire application, processes the request, and then shuts down the execution environment, ensuring a stateless handling of requests.

OpenSwoole, however, takes a different approach by keeping the application loaded in memory. It keeps the application in memory once started, and subsequent requests are handled within this persistent environment. This approach leads to significant performance improvements as the overhead of reloading the application for each request is eliminated. However, it also introduces new considerations for data management within your application.

With the application always loaded in memory, developers must exercise extra caution regarding data management. Different from the stateless nature of PHP-FPM, OpenSwoole's stateful environment can lead to data leaks if global or static variables are not correctly managed. This means that objects or data stored in memory persist across multiple requests, which can inadvertently lead to memory bloat or unintentional data exposure.

> **Important**: *Always ensure that objects, especially those containing sensitive data, are adequately destroyed after use to prevent memory leaks and potential security vulnerabilities.*

The tradeoff

As you might have predicted, the advantage of having the application loaded in memory comes with a tradeoff. The server reloading must be managed when changes are made to the application code. In PHP-FPM, code changes are reflected with each new request since the application environment is reinitialized every time. In contrast, with OpenSwoole, changes to the code require a server reload to refresh the files in memory and reflect the updated code. This introduces a new dynamic in the development workflow where developers must adopt strategies for efficiently managing code updates.

One common approach to handle this in OpenSwoole is "hot reload" strategies. Hot reload allows developers to reload the server automatically or manually to apply code changes without restarting the entire application. This can significantly enhance the development experience by reducing downtime and enabling quicker iterations.

Overall, while OpenSwoole offers performance and efficiency benefits over PHP-FPM by maintaining a persistent in-memory application state, it also requires developers to adopt new practices for data management and server reloading. Understanding these differences and incorporating best practices will ensure a smooth transition and optimal use of OpenSwoole in your PHP applications.

Hot Reload

PHP OpenSwoole operates with a different approach compared to traditional PHP setups, like PHP-FPM. In OpenSwoole, data can be shared between requests, enabling data reuse. Once the application is loaded into memory, it remains there and does not need to reload for every incoming request. The system becomes significantly faster since reloading the entire application for each request is unnecessary. However, as mentioned in the previous section, this also introduces some trade-offs:

1. We must handle specific actions differently to ensure data is not accidentally shared between requests.
2. During development, after changing the source code, you need strategies like "hot reloading" to see the updated version of the application without restarting the server manually for every change.

Hot reloading is a strategy used to automatically restart the OpenSwoole server whenever source code files are modified, enabling developers to see changes in real-time without manually restarting the server for each update. The OpenSwoole server includes built-in configurations specifically for reloading, which can reload the code beyond the server's code. However, because the server is programmatically built within the PHP application using OpenSwoole, any changes to the server code are integral to the application and require an external approach.

To entirely refresh the application, including any modifications to the server code, developers need to employ hot reload strategies beyond the native capabilities of OpenSwoole. This is where tools like Inotify or fswatch come into play. These tools monitor the file system for changes and trigger a server restart when necessary. While OpenSwoole can handle basic server reloading, using an external hot reload setup ensures that all aspects of the application, including the dynamically constructed server, are correctly reloaded to reflect the latest code changes.

In the subsequent paragraphs, we will explore these external tools in more detail. For example, Inotify[1] is a file change notification system for Unix systems, and fswatch[2] is a similar tool that can be used if your operating system does not support Inotify. Both of these tools can watch for changes in the file system and trigger the necessary actions to restart the OpenSwoole server, ensuring that the entire application, including its server component, is

[1] https://www.kernel.org/doc/html/latest/filesystems/inotify.html
[2] https://manpages.debian.org/testing/fswatch/fswatch.7.en.html

up-to-date with the latest code changes. This approach provides a robust solution for maintaining an efficient and responsive development workflow.

You can find more detailed information on this process at OpenSwoole's official documentation[3]. It involves adding a small component to watch the file system and triggering a server reload when changes are detected.

Let's start with the following server sample (Listing 3.2) and then we will explore the Docker environment and the hot reload script in more detail:

```php
<?php

use OpenSwoole\HTTP\Server;
use OpenSwoole\Http\Request;
use OpenSwoole\Http\Response;

if (!defined('PID_FILE')) {
    define('PID_FILE', './http-server-pid');
}

if (file_exists(PID_FILE)) {
    unlink(PID_FILE);
}

$server = new Server('0.0.0.0', 8001);

$server->on('start', function (Server $server) {
    file_put_contents(PID_FILE, $server->master_pid);
    echo 'HTTP server available at http://127.0.0.1:9503 (PID ' . $server->master_pid . ')' . PHP_EOL;
});

$server->on('request', function (Request $request, Response $response) {
    echo 'Incoming connection time: ' . date('Y-m-d H:i:s') . PHP_EOL;
    echo 'Incoming connection uri: ' . $request->server['request_uri'] . PHP_EOL;
    $response->header('Content-Type', 'text/plain');
    $response->end('Server response content.');
});

$server->on('close', function (Server $server) {
    echo 'Connection closed.\n';
});

$server->start();
```

[3] https://openswoole.com/docs/modules/swoole-server-reload

In the next chapter, we will delve deeper into the OpenSwoole HTTP Server, further exploring its features. The server example in Listing 3.2 will display loaded files in the command line after it reloads due to the signal sent by the Inotify script in Listing 3.1. This server registers the current server PID in the file specified by the `PID_FILE` constant.

If you only need to reload files included after the server starts, you can use the following server setting: `$server->set(['reload_async' => true])`. Add this before the `$server->start()` method. You can read more about it https://openswoole.com/docs/modules/swoole-server/configuration#reload_async.

The following section on Docker will explore how to set up a development environment with OpenSwoole and Docker. This section will introduce an alternative method for hot-reloading. This method is used because strategies with more complex dependencies are better handled in environments like Docker.

Docker

The PHP OpenSwoole project offers various useful repositories that can assist in addressing a wide range of issues. Among their many examples is an environment using Docker, a technology that has become ubiquitous due to its portability across multiple operating systems. One of the initial suggestions in their documentation is to explore the repository at OpenSwoole Docker[4]. This repository is an essential reference for working with OpenSwoole and Docker, providing examples for all PHP versions and covering both production and development environments.

The mentioned repository includes a Docker image file that helps you quickly set up an environment where you can start using OpenSwoole. Each branch corresponds to a different PHP version, allowing you to configure a development environment tailored to your needs. For production, you require a more specialized environment with tools for monitoring, whereas for development, a more flexible setup is often preferable. The examples directory will guide you through various configurations and use cases.

Despite the advanced nature of these configurations, it is beneficial to build your version of the container to understand how the different components interact. This hands-on approach helps grasp the setup's intricacies and provides insights into optimizing it for specific requirements.

For development purposes, the following git repository demonstrates how to implement hot reloading, as discussed in the section on Hot Reload: Jacked PHP Book Examples[5], specifically in the "03-examples" directory. Here is a sample Dockerfile for this case:

```
FROM openswoole/swoole:php8.3

ARG ENVIRONMENT_NAME

COPY ./rootfilesystem/ /

RUN chmod +x /entrypoint.sh

ENTRYPOINT ["/entrypoint.sh"]

WORKDIR "/var/www/html"
```

[4] https://openswoole.com/docs/get-started/try-docker
[5] https://github.com/Jacked-PHP/jacked-php-book-examples

The entrypoint script for the Dockerfile above is detailed in Listing 3.4:

```
#!/usr/bin/env bash

# Start the supervisor program.
/usr/bin/supervisord -c /etc/supervisor/conf.d/supervisord.conf &

WORK_DIR=$1
if [ ! -n "${WORK_DIR}" ] ;then
    WORK_DIR="."
fi

echo "Starting inotifywait..."

LOCKING=0 # Used to block the signal if it is not needed.

inotifywait --event modify --event create --event move --event delete -mrq ${WORK_DIR} | while read file

do
    if [[ ! ${file} =~ .php$ ]] ;then
        continue
    fi
    if [ ${LOCKING} -eq 1 ] ;then
        echo "Reloading, skipped."
        continue
    fi
    echo "File ${file} has been modified."
    LOCKING=1

    kill -9 $(cat ./http-server-pid) # kill the server.

    # Remove the server pid file to avoid problems when restarting the server.
    rm -f ./http-server-pid
    rm -f ./supervisord.pid

    sleep 2

    LOCKING=0
done

exit 0
```

The core of this setup is the `./docker/swoole/rootfilesystem` directory, which you can find in both the example repository and the official `docker-swoole` repository. This directory contains essential assets, such as supervisor configurations, which are copied into the container, enabling a robust and functional development environment.

> *Notice that in this container environment, sending the signal* `-9` *(SIGKILL) to Supervisor will simply restart the application. For every file change, you can send this signal to kill the existing server process, ensuring that changes are applied immediately.*

One issue to be aware of is the PID file verification. This file confirms the presence of a running server and its PID. If the service dies and the PID file is not removed, the restart process will encounter problems. Adapting this approach to handle such scenarios might be better if you anticipate this happening frequently.

> **127.0.0.1 or 0.0.0.0?** *The server in this repository exposes itself to external requests (0.0.0.0) rather than just localhost (127.0.0.1). This exposure is crucial because the example runs within a Docker container. When accessing the service through your browser, the connection comes from outside the container, requiring the server to accept external requests.*

You need Docker and docker-compose installed on your machine to utilize this setup. Assuming you are running this in a Linux environment, follow these steps to get the container up and running:

1. Clone the repository:
   `git clone https://github.com/Jacked-PHP/jacked-php-book-examples.git swoole-docker-base`
2. Navigate to the cloned directory:
   `cd swoole-docker-base/03-examples`
3. Execute the Docker command:
   `docker-compose up -d`
4. Once the container is built, you can navigate to http://localhost:8001 in your browser to see the server running:

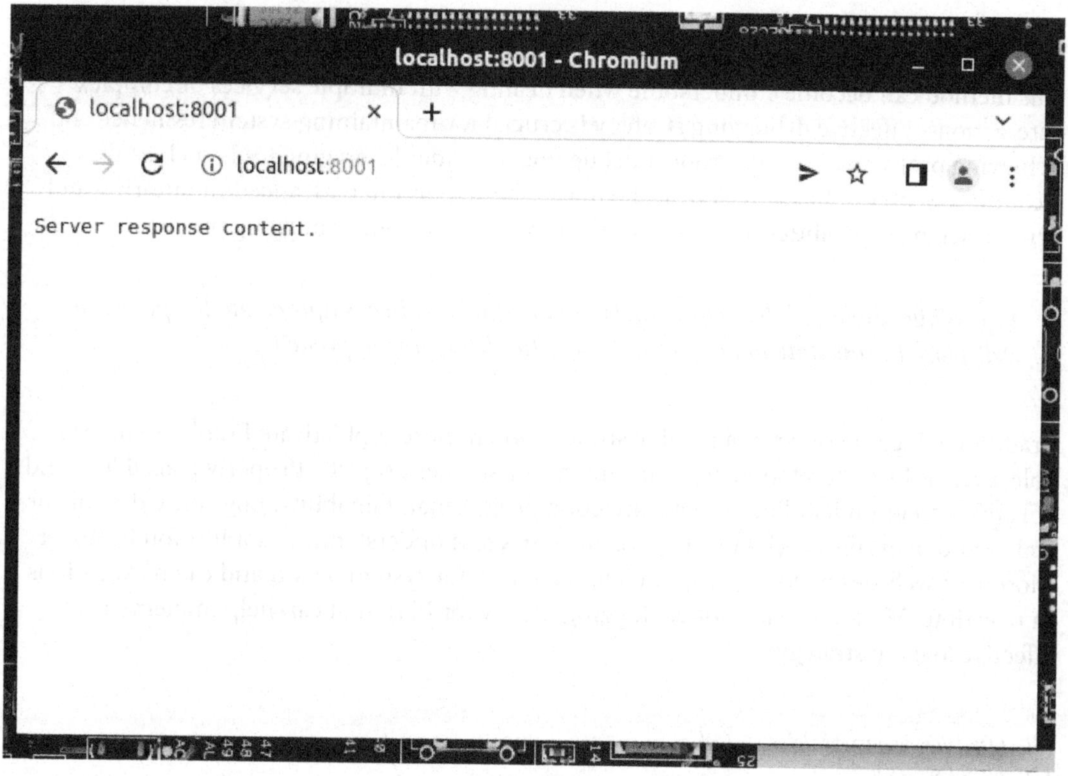

Figure 3.1: Screen of the server running within Docker.

Debugging

As mentioned earlier, PHP OpenSwoole alters the architectural design of your application when building with PHP. This section will explore some practical aspects of working within this new architecture, focusing on debugging strategies.

The first thing to remember is that the OpenSwoole server handles output differently compared to traditional PHP setups. Suppose your application encounters a dying statement (e.g., using `die()` or `exit()`); the output will not appear in the browser if you are running an HTTP server. Instead, these messages will be displayed in the command line where the OpenSwoole server is running. This is an important distinction, as it means you'll need to monitor the command line output to catch these errors. In contrast, standard output functions like `echo` and `var_dump()` will behave as expected, appearing in the browser for HTTP servers or the console for command line services.

While using `var_dump()` and `echo` statements is a common strategy to inspect variable values, this method can become cumbersome when dealing with multiple services or complex interactions. Effective debugging strategy is crucial for maintaining system resilience and achieving project success. For robust debugging, consider leveraging tools such as ElasticStack[6], Sentry[7], Bugsnag[8], or DataDog[9]. These tools offer advanced monitoring and error-tracking capabilities that can significantly enhance your debugging process.

> **Tip**: *While advanced debugging tools are invaluable, always appreciate the power of well-placed print statements and a thoughtful debugging approach.*

Traditional logging remains a reliable strategy when more sophisticated tools are unavailable, such as local development environments or smaller projects. Properly placed logs and effective exception handling can ensure good project maintainability. Logs provide a historical record of events crucial for diagnosing issues and understanding application behavior. Moreover, well-designed logging can help you monitor system health and catch exceptions in real-time. Monolog[10] is a robust logging library for PHP that can help implement an effective logging strategy.

---

[6] https://www.elastic.co/elastic-stack
[7] https://sentry.io
[8] https://www.bugsnag.com
[9] https://www.datadoghq.com
[10] https://github.com/Seldaek/monolog

Consider the following tips when setting up logging and debugging in PHP OpenSwoole:

1. **Use Structured Logging**: Structured logs are more accessible to parse and analyze, especially when dealing with large volumes of data. Monolog supports JSON formatting, which can be very useful.
2. **Log Levels**: Utilize different log levels (e.g., DEBUG, INFO, WARNING, ERROR) to categorize log messages. This helps filter and prioritize log data.
3. **Centralized Logging**: Consider aggregating logs from multiple services into a central repository for production environments. Tools like ElasticStack or DataDog can help with this. Only make sure that they are filterable.
4. **Exception Handling**: Implement robust exception handling to capture and log unexpected errors. Ensure that sensitive information is not exposed in logs.
5. **Performance Monitoring**: Use performance monitoring tools to identify bottlenecks and optimize system performance.

Let's look at a basic example of setting up Monolog for logging in a PHP OpenSwoole application:

```php
<?php
use Monolog\Logger;
use Monolog\Handler\StreamHandler;

// Create the logger
$logger = new Logger('my_logger');

// Now add some handlers
$logger->pushHandler(new StreamHandler(__DIR__.'/logs/app.log', Logger::DEBUG));

// You can now use your logger
$logger->info('This is a log message!');
$logger->error('This is an error message!');
```

This example sets up a Monolog logger that writes log messages to a file called `app.log`. The log level is set to DEBUG, meaning all messages at this level and above (INFO, WARNING, ERROR, etc.) will be logged.

In summary, while debugging in PHP OpenSwoole may require adapting to its architectural nuances, employing effective strategies and tools can significantly streamline the process. Whether using advanced monitoring tools or traditional logging, maintaining a robust debugging setup is essential for developing resilient and reliable applications.

Composer

In the contemporary software development landscape, utilizing PHP Composer packages has emerged as an optimal approach for PHP-based software creation. Composer, the package manager, provides numerous advantages, including dependency management, automatic dependency loading, script management, and application installer functionalities.

To comprehensively understand Composer, refer to its official website: Composer[11].

Composer's widespread adoption equips developers with enhanced capabilities, facilitating swifter and more efficient development processes. One of Composer's key strengths is its ability to manage dependencies effectively. By defining dependencies in a `composer.json` file, developers can ensure that all required packages are automatically loaded, reducing the time and effort needed to handle dependencies manually. This streamlined approach accelerates development and minimizes the risk of version conflicts and other dependency-related issues.

Another significant advantage of Composer is its support for script management. Developers can define custom scripts in the `composer.json` file to automate everyday tasks, such as running tests, generating documentation, or deploying applications. This feature enhances productivity by enabling developers to focus on coding rather than repetitive tasks.

Moreover, Composer fosters the creation and utilization of reusable components. By leveraging existing packages from the Composer ecosystem, developers can avoid reinventing the wheel and instead build on the work of others. This approach aligns with the principles of the Open Source community, promoting collaboration and knowledge sharing. To contribute to or source packages, visit Packagist[12], the default package repository for Composer. A self-hosted version of Packagist is available for organizations with specific hosting needs, detailed at Packagist.com[13].

Throughout this book, our examples will assume the presence of a Composer environment. Each example includes a `composer.json` file listing all dependencies, ensuring you can easily replicate the setup. Even if you prefer not to dive into the git repositories immediately, you can identify dependencies using the code examples' namespaces.

---

[11] https://getcomposer.org/
[12] https://packagist.org/
[13] https://packagist.com/

To get started with Composer, follow these steps:

1. **Install Composer**: Download and install Composer from the official website. Detailed instructions for various operating systems are available on the Composer installation page[14].
2. **Initialize a Project**: Use the command `composer init` to create a new `composer.json` file in your project directory. This file will serve as the blueprint for managing your project's dependencies.
3. **Add Dependencies**: Use the command `composer require <package-name>` to add dependencies to your project. Composer will update the `composer.json` file and install the specified packages.
4. **Autoloading**: Composer provides an autoloading mechanism, eliminating the need for manual `require` or `include` statements. Include the following line in your PHP script to enable autoloading:
   ```
   require 'vendor/autoload.php';
   ```
5. **Update Dependencies:** Use `composer update` to update all packages to their latest versions based on the version constraints defined in `composer.json`. It ensures that your project benefits from the latest improvements and security patches.
6. **Script Management**: Define custom scripts in the `composer.json` file under the `scripts` section. For example:
   ```
   "scripts": {
       "test": "phpunit",
       "start": "php -S localhost:8000 -t public"
   }
   ```
   These scripts can be executed using `composer run-script <script-name>`.

Integrating Composer into your development workflow allows you to streamline dependency management, automate repetitive tasks, and leverage a vast ecosystem of reusable components. It enhances productivity and promotes best practices and collaboration within the PHP development community.

---

[14] https://getcomposer.org/doc/00-intro.md

Extra Considerations

While it has been announced that OpenSwoole will eventually support XDebug, this functionality was unavailable when this book was written. The OpenSwoole documentation (https://openswoole.com/tools) currently advises against using step debugging due to the asynchronous nature of the framework. However, tools and methods are available to adapt the current version of OpenSwoole for step debugging if necessary.

> **Important:** *Visit OpenSwoole Tools[15] for a collection of valuable tools to assist with your day-to-day work with OpenSwoole.*

Other debuggers and debugging tools are continually being developed within the community. It's essential to stay informed about these advancements, as they can provide new and improved ways to debug your applications.

Setting up an effective development environment for asynchronous programming or event-based architectures often relies heavily on traditional logging. Logs provide a straightforward way to trace the execution flow and capture the application's state at various points. While basic logging can be very effective, advanced tools can enhance log visualization and analysis, providing deeper insights into application behavior.

[15] https://openswoole.com/tools

Chapter 4

Setting up a Web Server with PHP OpenSwoole

Examples of this chapter: https://phpa.me/jacked-php-chapter-4

The majority of applications built with PHP are made for the web. When not for the web, they run on machines as services for many different purposes, from applications that automatically dispatch emails to database monitors that generate reports and alerts.

Here we will see cases for TCP servers focused on HTTP connections, mainly for the web. As known, HTTP is a TCP/IP text-based communication with a header and body [1]. Usually, the header carries things like cookies, authorization tokens, and metadata about the content of that request/response. The details are abstracted in the protocol, so you only need

[1] *HTTP 1.1 Reference: https://datatracker.ietf.org/doc/html/rfc2616*

to care about some aspects if you are working at a deeper level of the operational system or want specific behaviors with the application.

PHP standing alone

The usual way of running PHP applications is to have sequential code where each step is accomplished before the next one until you reach the end of the code. With that in mind, every time you write a PHP script, the last line of that script is expected to be executed last. With OpenSwoole, we use callbacks that executes whenever given events happen via sub-processes. The server itself is a group of sub-processes running as a callback to events under the master process, which is the executing script. That said, OpenSwoole has some pre-established events that you can use to customize the server's behavior.

To see the entire list of events that can be used to customize the server, visit the documentation https://openswoole.com/docs/modules/swoole-server-on.

Even though we have many options for server customization, we only need some of them. To understand each event, you might want to check the `OpenSwoole\Server` interface, which is the base of other server classes in OpenSwoole - the TCP server from which all other server implementations inherit. Here is its documentation:

https://openswoole.com/docs/modules/swoole-server-doc

To understand it further, with motivation and more, you can visit the documentation or even go to the more specialized book Mastering Swoole PHP[2]. For the basic functionalities of our server, we will consider the following code snippet:

```
1. <?php
2.
3. use OpenSwoole\HTTP\Server;
4. use OpenSwoole\Http\Request;
5. use OpenSwoole\Http\Response;
6.
7. $server = new Server("127.0.0.1", 9503);
8.
9. $server->on("start", function (Server $server) {
10.     echo "HTTP server available at http://127.0.0.1:9503\n";
11. });
12.
13. $server->on("request", function (Request $request, Response $response) {
14.     echo "Incoming connection time: " . date('Y-m-d H:i:s') . PHP_EOL;
15.     echo "Incoming connection uri: " . $request->server['request_uri'] . PHP_EOL;
16.     $response->header("Content-Type", "text/plain");
17.     $response->end("Here it all starts.\n");
18. });
19.
20. $server->start();
```

Reference in the repo: https://phpa.me/jacked-php-chapter-4-http_server

As you can see in Listing 4.1, we are customizing only two events: `start` and `request`. The `start` event's callback will be triggered when you start the server. For every request received, the `request` event will be triggered.

At line 7, we start the server specifying the IP address and the port. In line 9, we register a callback to customize what to do when the server starts (the `start` event) - this is not essential, but it is always a good practice to show something that confirms that the server has started. At line 13, we register a callback for the `request` event. Within its callback, we display the current time and the request URI. In line 16, we have a header added to the response; in line 17, we ended the response by adding its body content. In line 20, we finally start the server, which will keep running until we kill the master process (possibly, at the console, by typing CTRL+C or by killing the service by the PID - remember the hot-reload strategy covered in the last chapter? This is the same PID).

[2] https://swoolebook.com/

To start the server, you need to run this in the command line (considering that the filename is `http_server.php`:

```
php http_server.php
```

The output for this given server, while running this command on the terminal, is as shown in Figure 4.1:

Figure 4.1: The output when running the HTTP server script.

In Figure 4.2, you'll be able to see the terminal's output when receiving a request at Listing 4.1:

Figure 4.2: The output when receiving a request at the http server.

In the browser, you'll see what is shown in Figure 4.3:

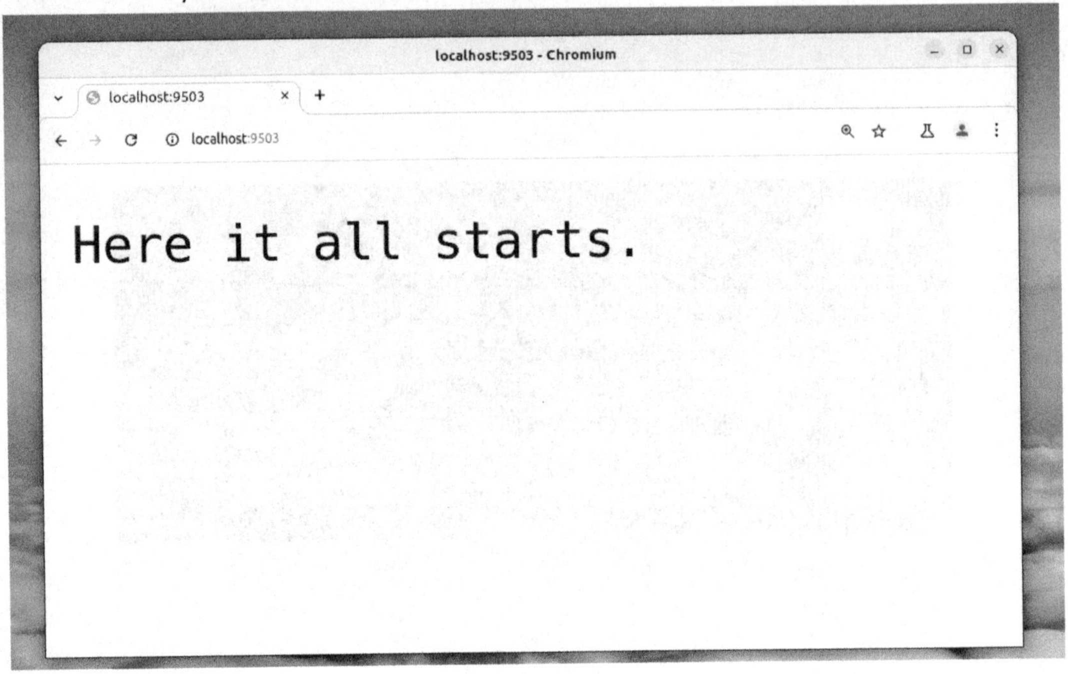

Figure 4.3 - Server output in the browser

> *Note: an essential aspect of OpenSwoole Servers is that there are two modes of running it: OpenSwoole::SIMPLE_MODE and OpenSwoole::POOL_MODE. In Simple Mode, one process runs everything, and the reactor thread process all the incoming requests. New processes are spawned to process each incoming request in the Pool Mode. We won't go too deep into the weeds here, but if you want to learn more, you'll dive into Linux and C++ programming and read some of the source code of OpenSwoole. That requires a more specialized understanding of Linux servers and processes, again, a subject for the previously referred book[https://swoolebook.com/]. This book covers the Multi-Process Mode mode, which is the default one (`OpenSwoole\Server::POOL_MODE`). The "mode" is the third parameter at the `OpenSwoole\Http\Server` class constructor (e.g., `$server = new Server("127.0.0.1", 9503, OpenSwoole\Server::POOL_MODE);`).*

You might have noticed that the server is just showing plain text. The reason for that is, as you can see in line 16 of Listing 4.1, that the `Content Type` header is set to `text/plain`. There is a way for us to display HTML instead. For such, we can do something like in Listing 4.2:

```php
<?php

use OpenSwoole\HTTP\Server;
use OpenSwoole\Http\Request;
use OpenSwoole\Http\Response;

$server = new Server("127.0.0.1", 9503);

$server->on("start", function (Server $server) {
    echo "HTTP server available at http://127.0.0.1:9503\n";
});

$server->on("request", function (Request $request, Response $response) {
    echo "Incoming connection time: " . date('Y-m-d H:i:s') . PHP_EOL;
    echo "Incoming connection uri: " . $request->server['request_uri'] . PHP_EOL;

    $html_content = <<<HTML
<html>
<head>
    <meta charset="UTF-8" />
    <title>HTML Swoole Server</title>
</head>
<body>
    <h1>My Page Title</h1>
    <div>The page's Body goes here</div>
</body>
</html>
HTML;

    $response->header("Content-Type", "text/html");
    $response->header("Charset", "UTF-8");
    $response->end($html_content);
});

$server->on('close', function ($server) {
    echo "Connection closed.\n";
});

$server->start();
```

Reference in the repo: https://phpa.me/jacked-php-chapter-4-http_server_2

Listing 4.2 is the same as Listing 4.1, but instead of serving plain text, it servers HTML code. The browser view would be like in Figure 4.4:

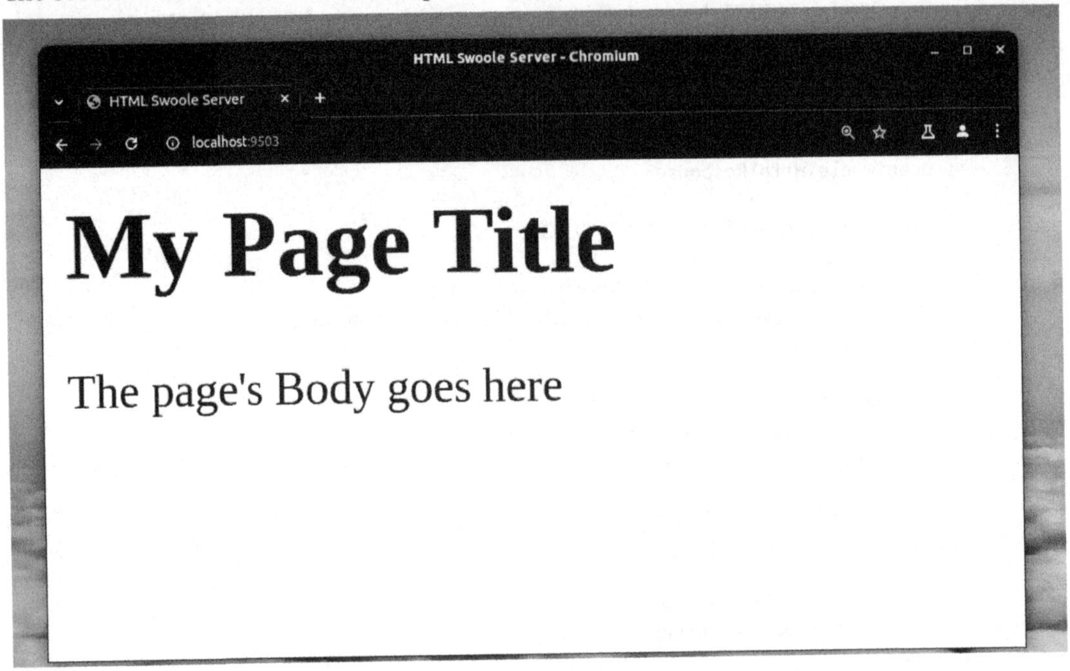

Figure 4.4: Server output in the browser with HTML content.

Building a Small Application

There are better ways to server HTML templates than writing the code in the callback closure. A different way would be using a template engine to serve HTML content. This is present in Listing 4.3.

Reference in the repo: https://phpa.me/jacked-php-chapter-4-http_server_3

```php
<?php
require __DIR__ . '/vendor/autoload.php';

use OpenSwoole\HTTP\Server;
use OpenSwoole\Http\Request;
use OpenSwoole\Http\Response;
use League\Plates\Engine;
use Dotenv\Dotenv;

$dotenv = Dotenv::createImmutable(__DIR__);
$dotenv->load();

$server_address = $_ENV['SERVER_ADDRESS'] ?? '127.0.0.1';
$server_port = $_ENV['SERVER_PORT'] ?? '9503';

$server = new Server($server_address, $server_port);

$server->on("start", function (Server $server) use ($server_address, $server_port) {
    echo "HTTP server available at http://" . $server_address . ":" . $server_port . PHP_EOL;
});

$server->on("request", function (Request $request, Response $response) {
    echo "Incoming connection time: " . date('Y-m-d H:i:s') . PHP_EOL;
    echo "Incoming connection uri: " . $request->server['request_uri'] . PHP_EOL;

    $custom_content = '';
    if (null !== $request->get && isset($request->get['content'])) {
        $custom_content = $request->get['content'];
    }

    $templates = new Engine(__DIR__ . '/html');
    $html_content = $templates->render('sample1', [
        'main_heading' => 'My Page Title',
        'content' => 'The page\'s Body goes here... ' . $custom_content,
    ]);

    $response->header("Content-Type", "text/html");
    $response->header("Charset", "UTF-8");
    $response->end($html_content);
});

$server->on('close', function ($server) {
    echo "Connection closed.\n";
});

$server->start();
```

This version of the server would present precisely the same way as before in the browser but with a few advantages. Before we jump into the benefits, at this version, we have a composer being used to load 2 dependencies: Plates and Dotenv. Plates is one of the many packages from the group of developers named ^The PHP League[3]. In the example project directory for this chapter, you'll see the complete example, but you can also follow the instructions at the Plates site: https://platesphp.com/[4]. On the other hand, the Dotenv library (https://github.com/vlucas/phpdotenv[5] is used to load environment variables from the file `.env`, which is usually used to set sensitive information that will not be stored with the source code in the Version Control system (e.g., Git).

> **Important**: *it is essential to note that we use some autoloading PSR-4 strategy from composer for these examples. You can get more information about it here: https://getcomposer.org/doc/04-schema.md#autoload.*

The autoloading for dependencies via composer makes it very easy to use libraries without including their files manually.

In line 3 of Listing 4.3, the composer autoload is in place. This line loads all the dependencies installed via composer (but you can also use it to load your source code using some PSR-4, which you can find more about here: https://getcomposer.org/doc/01-basic-usage.md#autoloading). In line 11, we use the Dotenv library to load information from a file called `.env`. Right after that, on line 14, we verify if the server address and port are set; if not, we specify default parameters. In line 27, we define a variable that can be customized by using a GET parameter called `content`, and then we access the attribute `$request->get` to have access to it - notice that its default value is `null`. In case you need another type of information from the `Request` object, you can check the OpenSwoole documentation here: https://openswoole.com/docs/modules/swoole-http-request[6]. If that is set, we update the variable `$custom_content`, otherwise we leave it empty. To see that affecting the content, you need to load a URL like this: `http://127.0.0.1:9503/?content=the%20custom%20part`. This URL containing the content GET parameter would result in what you can see in Figure 4.5:

[3] *https://thephpleague.com/*
[4] *https://platesphp.com/*
[5] *https://github.com/vlucas/phpdotenv*
[6] *https://openswoole.com/docs/modules/swoole-http-request*

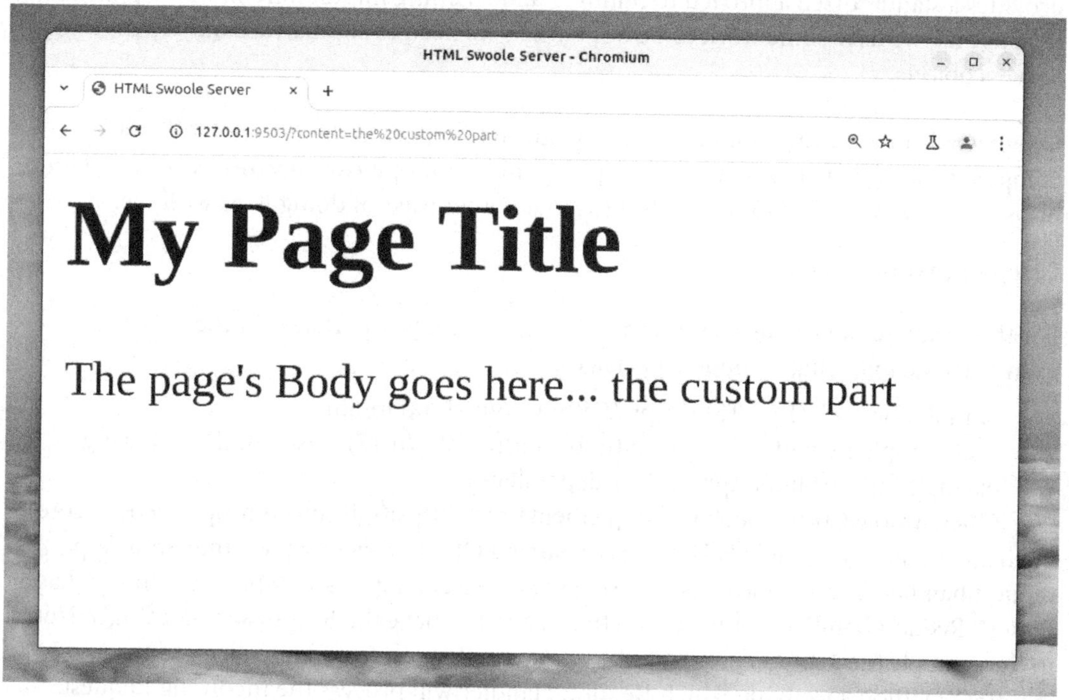

Figure 4.5: Server output in the browser with HTML content with dynamic information and using a PHP template library.

Making Request PSR-7 compatible

When working on projects where other developers will work on or code that will be reused and shared, it becomes essential to make it in a way that people can understand what is happening with a smaller learning curve. That is one of the advantages of having standards: to avoid confusion and to make processes more streamlined in human activities. Standard practices also benefit projects in quality. With that in mind, having our requests in the same expected format as the rest of the typical PHP applications is an excellent idea. This lack of consistency is when PHP-FIG standard recommendations come into place.

It happens that the OpenSwoole Request object has a different interface than PSR-7[7] or PSR-15[8], standards used for HTTP requests and responses, and in request handlers. The PSR-7 provides a standardized way to work with HTTP messages in PHP. The PSR-15

[7] https://www.php-fig.org/psr/psr-7/
[8] https://www.php-fig.org/psr/psr-15/

provides a standardized approach to building and chaining middleware in PHP applications. Due to that, we have some work to be done when we need to standardize our OpenSwoole Servers objects.

OpenSwoole in 2022 (in version 22.0.0) introduced support to the referred PSR via a composer package openswoole/core (https://github.com/openswoole/core , documentation: https://openswoole.com/docs/psr). But there are other ways of doing it, as we'll see.

Using openswoole/core

For this example, we will be using (other than the composer packages in the previous examples) the following composer packages:

- Slim Framework (PSR-15) (https://github.com/slimphp/Slim)
- PSR-7 implementation (https://github.com/nyholm/psr7) - used in the following example for the Slim's App PSR-17 dependency.
- OpenSwoole Core - for PSR-7 implementation (https://github.com/openswoole/core)

Listing 4.4.1 shows a simple HTTP Server parsing OpenSwoole Request into Slim App request handler. The `Slim\App` class is also a `RequestHandlerInterface` implementation. It has a PSR-17 Request handler that processes the Request to have the Response accordingly. Note in the example the `Slim\App` proxying the incoming Request to a Controller and the `$server->handle()` method specifying which Request Handler will process the incoming Request:

Reference in the repo: https://phpa.me/jacked-php-chapter-4-http_server_4_core

```php
<?php
const ROOT_DIR = __DIR__;
require __DIR__ . '/vendor/autoload.php';

use App\Http\Controllers\IndexController;
use Dotenv\Dotenv;
use Slim\App;
use Nyholm\Psr7\Factory\Psr17Factory;
use OpenSwoole\HTTP\Server;
use Psr\Http\Message\ServerRequestInterface;

// Load config.

$dotenv = Dotenv::createImmutable(__DIR__);
$dotenv->load();

// Section: Start Request Handler (Slim).

$app = new App(new Psr17Factory());
$app->get('/', [IndexController::class, 'index']);
$app->addRoutingMiddleware();

// OpenSwoole part.

$server_address = $_ENV['SERVER_ADDRESS'] ?? '127.0.0.1';
$server_port = $_ENV['SERVER_PORT'] ?? '9503';

$server = new Server($server_address, $server_port);

$server->set([
    'document_root' => __DIR__ . '/public',
    'enable_static_handler' => true,
    'static_handler_locations' => ['/imgs'],
]);

$server->on("start", function (Server $server) use ($server_address, $server_port) {
    echo "HTTP server available at http://" . $server_address . ":" . $server_port . PHP_EOL;
});

$server->handle(fn (ServerRequestInterface $request) => $app->handle($request));

$server->on('close', function ($server) {
    echo "Connection closed.\n";
});

$server->start();
```

> *This example won't work in an OpenSwoole version before 22.0.0.*

Lines 30-32 are the standard way to start the Slim App. The special piece that differs from the following example is line 40. That line shows the usage of the `$server->handle()` method. That method specifies a PSR-15 handler to handle the incoming Request processing.

Using Slim Framework libraries

For this, we will be using the following libraries (composer packages):

- SwoolePsr7 (https://github.com/iLexN/swoole-psr7)
- Slim Framework (https://github.com/slimphp/Slim)
- PSR-7 implementation (https://github.com/nyholm/psr7)

Listing 4.4 shows a simple HTTP Server parsing OpenSwoole Request into Slim App request handler. The `Slim\App` class is also a `RequestHandlerInterface` implementation. It has a Psr7 Request handler that processes the Request to have the Response accordingly. Notice that, in this example, we also have an autoload added to the `composer.json` file, as shown in Listing 4.6. To have the same model as before but proxying the incoming Request to a Controller following some standards, this is how it would be done:

```
1. <?php
2.
3. const ROOT_DIR = __DIR__;
4.
5. require __DIR__ . '/vendor/autoload.php';
6.
7. use App\Http\Controllers\IndexController;
8. use Dotenv\Dotenv;
9. use Ilex\SwoolePsr7\SwooleResponseConverter;
10. use Ilex\SwoolePsr7\SwooleServerRequestConverter;
11. use Slim\App;
12. use Nyholm\Psr7\Factory\Psr17Factory;
13. use OpenSwoole\HTTP\Server;
14. use OpenSwoole\Http\Request;
15. use OpenSwoole\Http\Response;
16.
17. // Load config.
18.
19. $dotenv = Dotenv::createImmutable(__DIR__);
20. $dotenv->load();
21.
22. // Section: Start Psr7 Converter.
23.
24. $psr17Factory = new Psr17Factory();
```

```
$requestConverter = new SwooleServerRequestConverter(
    $psr17Factory,
    $psr17Factory,
    $psr17Factory,
    $psr17Factory
);

// Section: Start Request Handler (Slim).

$app = new App($psr17Factory);
$app->get('/', [IndexController::class, 'index']);
$app->addRoutingMiddleware();

// Swoole part.

$server_address = isset($_ENV['SERVER_ADDRESS']) ? $_ENV['SERVER_ADDRESS'] : '127.0.0.1';
$server_port = isset($_ENV['SERVER_PORT']) ? $_ENV['SERVER_PORT'] : '9503';

$server = new Server($server_address, $server_port);

$server->set([
    'document_root' => __DIR__ . '/public',
    'enable_static_handler' => true,
    'static_handler_locations' => ['/imgs'],
]);

$server->on("start", function (Server $server) use ($server_address, $server_port) {
    echo "HTTP server available at http://" . $server_address . ":" . $server_port . PHP_EOL;
});

$server->on("request", function (Request $request, Response $response) use ($app, $requestConverter) {
    $psr7Request = $requestConverter->createFromSwoole($request);
    $psr7Response = $app->handle($psr7Request);
    $converter = new SwooleResponseConverter($response);
    $converter->send($psr7Response);
});

$server->on('close', function ($server) {
    echo "Connection closed.\n";
});

$server->start();
```

Reference in the repo: https://phpa.me/jacked-php-chapter-4-http_server_4_slim

Apart from the libraries mentioned before, what happened is that the code responsible for the Request handling at the `request` event content got moved to a controller by the Request Handler. Sections to notice that were added are "Section: Start Psr7 Converter" (line 31) and "Section: Start Request Handler (Slim)" (line 41).

In Listing 4.5, you can see the Controller:

```
<?php

namespace App\Http\Controllers;

use App\Http\Controllers\Traits\HasServerParams;
use Psr\Http\Message\ServerRequestInterface;
use Psr\Http\Message\ResponseInterface;
use League\Plates\Engine;

class IndexController
{
    use HasServerParams;

    public function index(ServerRequestInterface $request, ResponseInterface $response)
    {
        $serverParams = $this->getServerParams($request);

        echo "Incoming connection time: " . date('Y-m-d H:i:s') . PHP_EOL;
        echo "Incoming connection uri: " . $serverParams['request_uri'] ?? '' . PHP_EOL;

        $query = $request->getQueryParams();

        $templates = new Engine(ROOT_DIR . '/html');
        $html_content = $templates->render('sample4', [
            'main_heading' => 'My Page Title',
            'content' => 'The page\'s Body goes here... ' . ($query['content'] ?? ''),
        ]);

        $response->getBody()->write($html_content);
        return $response->withStatus(200);
    }
}
```

Reference in the repo: https://phpa.me/jacked-php-chapter-4-IndexController

In Listing 4.5.1 is the trait mentioned in the IndexController seen in the previous listing:

```php
<?php

namespace App\Http\Controllers\Traits;

use Psr\Http\Message\ServerRequestInterface;

trait HasServerParams
{
    protected function getServerParams(ServerRequestInterface $request)
    {
        $serverParams = [];
        foreach ($request->getServerParams() as $key => $value) {
            $serverParams[strtolower($key)] = $value;
        }
        return $serverParams;
    }
}
```

Reference in the repo: https://phpa.me/jacked-php-chapter-4-HasServerParams

```json
{
    "require": {
        "league/plates": "^3.4",
        "vlucas/phpdotenv": "^5.3",
        "ilexn/swoole-convert-psr7": "^0.6.0",
        "slim/slim": "^4.0",
        "nyholm/psr7": "^1.4",
        "slim/psr7": "^1.4",
        "lotharthesavior/chocookies": "^0.0.3",
        "ramsey/uuid": "^4.3",
        "psr/simple-cache": "^3.0",
        "openswoole/core": "^22.1",
        "openswoole/ide-helper": "^22.0",
        "ext-json": "*",
        "ext-curl": "*",
        "php": "^8"
    },
    "autoload": {
        "psr-4": {
            "App\\": "src/"
        }
    }
}
```

Reference in the repo: https://phpa.me/jacked-php-chapter-4-composer_json

With the given service, you'll find the outputs shown at the Terminal (Figure 4.6) and the Browser (Figure 4.7)

Figure 4.6: Terminal with Listing 4.4 output.

Figure 4.7: Browser with Listing 4.4 output.

Form Submission

A critical aspect of any app is the capacity to submit information to a server and then do something with it. The traditional way of doing such is through form submission.

We will add a new endpoint to the Request Handler for this example. Then, we will process the incoming request at the Controller we built in the last example, but this time in a new method. In this example, we will be adding a POST request workflow. The HTTP Verb (POST) will require a similar amount of work in this example because the request handler abstracts it.

In this case, we will add and submit a form, handling the data on the other side. We will be doing little with the data for simplicity. The code would be as shown in Listing 4.7:

```php
<?php

const ROOT_DIR = __DIR__;

require __DIR__ . '/vendor/autoload.php';

use App\Http\Controllers\IndexController;
use App\Http\Controllers\SubscriptionController;
use Dotenv\Dotenv;
use Ilex\SwoolePsr7\SwooleResponseConverter;
use Ilex\SwoolePsr7\SwooleServerRequestConverter;
use Slim\App;
use Nyholm\Psr7\Factory\Psr17Factory;
use OpenSwoole\HTTP\Server;
use OpenSwoole\Http\Request;
use OpenSwoole\Http\Response;

// Load config.

$dotenv = Dotenv::createImmutable(__DIR__);
$dotenv->load();

// Start Psr7 Converter.

$psr17Factory = new Psr17Factory();
$requestConverter = new SwooleServerRequestConverter(
    $psr17Factory,
    $psr17Factory,
    $psr17Factory,
    $psr17Factory
);

```

```php
// Start Request Handler (Slim).

$app = new App($psr17Factory);
$app->get('/', [IndexController::class, 'index']);
$app->get('/subscription', [SubscriptionController::class, 'subscriptionForm']);
$app->post('/subscription', [SubscriptionController::class, 'subscribe']);
$app->addRoutingMiddleware();

// Swoole part.

$server_address = $_ENV['SERVER_ADDRESS'] ?? '127.0.0.1';
$server_port = $_ENV['SERVER_PORT'] ?? '9503';

$server = new Server($server_address, $server_port);

$server->set([
    'document_root' => __DIR__ . '/public',
    'enable_static_handler' => true,
    'static_handler_locations' => ['/imgs'],
]);

$server->on("start", function (Server $server) use ($server_address, $server_port) {
    echo "HTTP server available at http://" . $server_address . ":" . $server_port . PHP_EOL;
});

$server->on("request", function (Request $request, Response $response) use ($app, $requestConverter) {
    $psr7Request = $requestConverter->createFromSwoole($request);
    $psr7Response = $app->handle($psr7Request);
    $converter = new SwooleResponseConverter($response);
    $converter->send($psr7Response);
});

$server->on('close', function ($server) {
    echo "Connection closed.\n";
});

$server->start();
```

Reference in the repo: https://phpa.me/jacked-php-chapter-4-http_server_5

For this example, we added the `SubscriptionController`. We add the methods `subscriptionForm` and `subscribe` to present and handle the incoming form (Listing 4.8).

```
<?php

namespace App\Http\Controllers;

use App\Http\Controllers\Traits\HasServerParams;
use Psr\Http\Message\ServerRequestInterface;
use Psr\Http\Message\ResponseInterface;
use League\Plates\Engine;

class SubscriptionController
{
    use HasServerParams;

    public function subscriptionForm(ServerRequestInterface $request, ResponseInterface $response)
    {
        $serverParams = $this->getServerParams($request);

        echo "Incoming connection time: " . date('Y-m-d H:i:s') . PHP_EOL;
        echo "Incoming connection uri: " . $serverParams['REQUEST_URI'] ?? '' . PHP_EOL;

        $templates = new Engine(ROOT_DIR . '/html');
        $html_content = $templates->render('sample5', [
            'main_heading' => 'Subscription Page',
        ]);

        $response->getBody()->write($html_content);
        return $response->withStatus(200);
    }

    public function subscribe(ServerRequestInterface $request, ResponseInterface $response)
    {
        $serverParams = $this->getServerParams($request);

        $data = $request->getParsedBody();

        echo "Incoming connection time: " . date('Y-m-d H:i:s') . PHP_EOL;
        echo "Incoming connection uri: " . $serverParams['REQUEST_URI'] ?? '' . PHP_EOL;
        echo "Incoming connection data: " . json_encode($data) . PHP_EOL;

```

```
        $templates = new Engine(ROOT_DIR . '/html');
        $html_content = $templates->render('sample5-result', [
            'main_heading' => 'Subscription Page Result',
            'email' => $data['email'],
        ]);

        $response->getBody()->write($html_content);
        return $response->withStatus(200);
    }
}
```

Reference in the repo: https://phpa.me/jacked-php-chapter-4-SubscriptionControllerV1

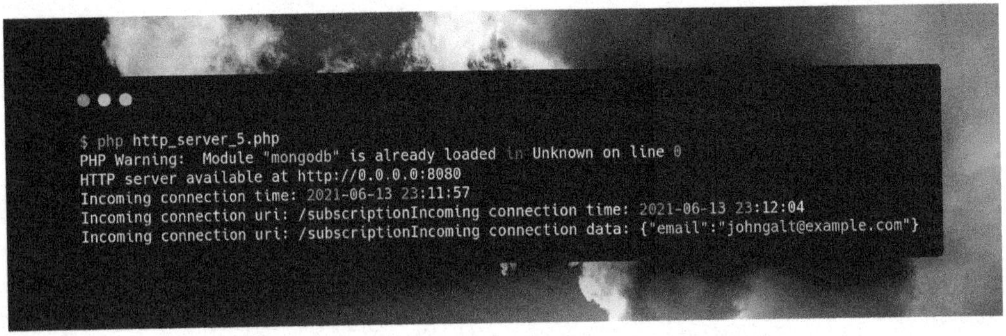

Figure 4.8: Terminal output for Listing 4.8 changes

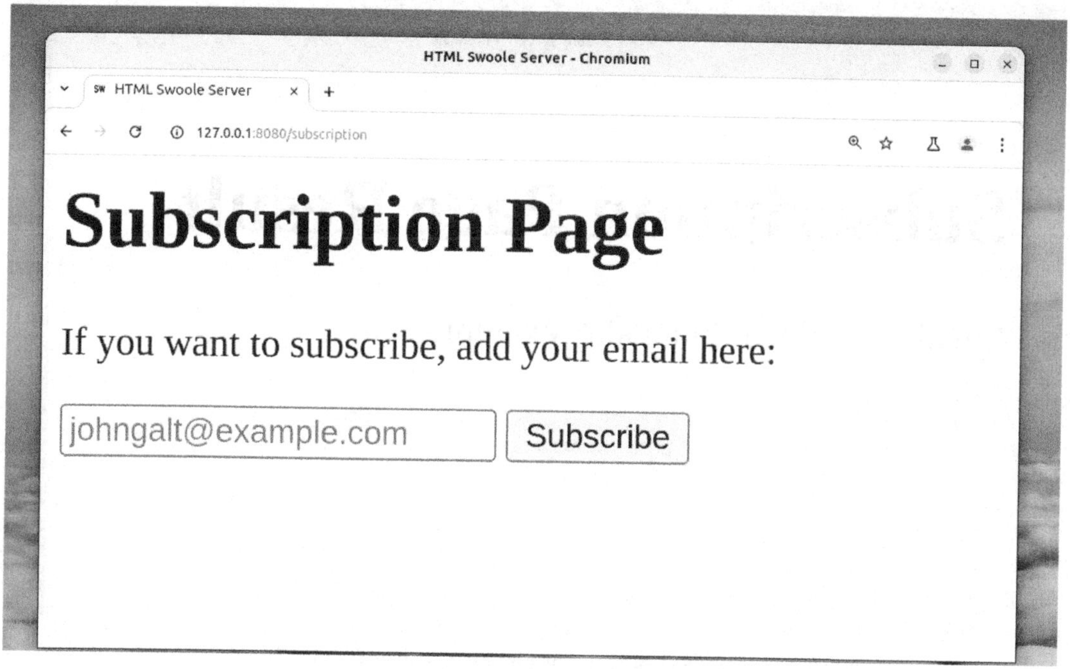

Figure 4.9: Browser output for Listing 4.8 before form submission

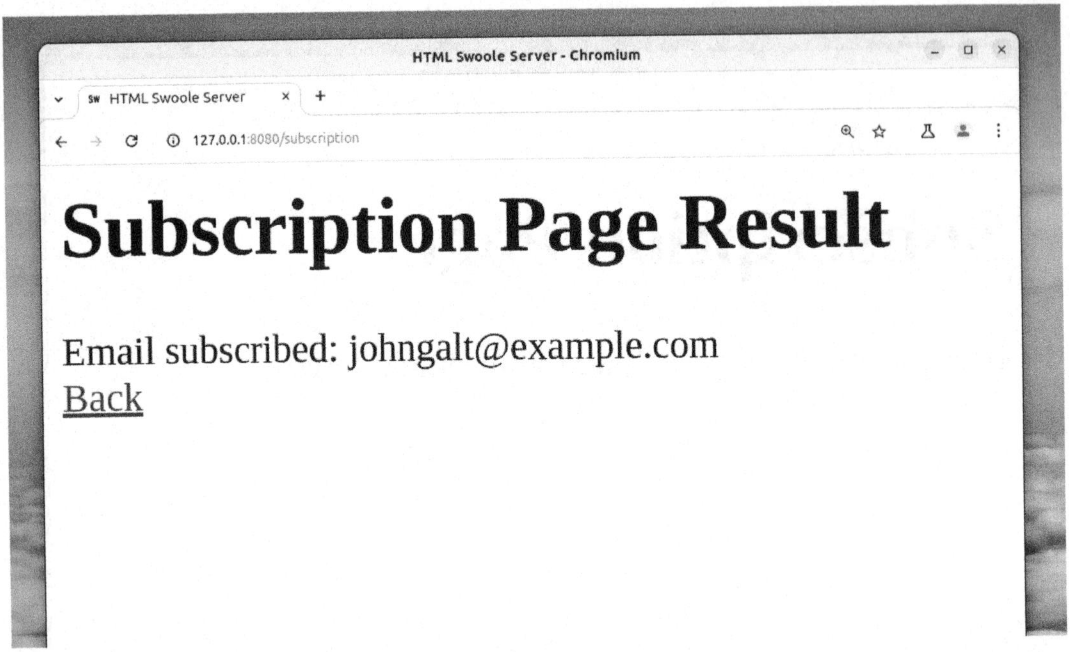

Figure 4.10: Browser output for Listing 4.8 after form submission

In this example, we are not saving the data, just executing a basic presentation logic with the incoming data.

Using Middleware

Let's enhance the service now with some validation. For that, we will use a middleware layer. Middleware will be used here to set some validation for the incoming data. The process will add a layer to validate the incoming request. Eventually, this can get more complex, like verifying authorization or further security checks.

Since we are using Slim for the examples, we will add the Middleware to the routes we want. According to the interface, we can also add it to a group of routes all at once, but for the sake of simplicity, we will be doing this just for the single routes for now: the `/subscription`.

Listing 4.9 shows the modified server example:

```php
<?php

const ROOT_DIR = __DIR__;

require __DIR__ . '/vendor/autoload.php';

use App\Http\Middlewares\ExampleMiddleware;
use App\Http\Controllers\IndexController;
use App\Http\Controllers\SubscriptionController;
use Dotenv\Dotenv;
use Ilex\SwoolePsr7\SwooleResponseConverter;
use Ilex\SwoolePsr7\SwooleServerRequestConverter;
use Slim\App;
use Nyholm\Psr7\Factory\Psr17Factory;
use OpenSwoole\HTTP\Server;
use OpenSwoole\Http\Request;
use OpenSwoole\Http\Response;

// Load config.

$dotenv = Dotenv::createImmutable(__DIR__);
$dotenv->load();

// Start Psr7 Converter.

$psr17Factory = new Psr17Factory();
$requestConverter = new SwooleServerRequestConverter(
    $psr17Factory,
    $psr17Factory,
    $psr17Factory,
    $psr17Factory
);

// Start Request Handler (Slim).

$app = new App($psr17Factory);
$app->get('/', [IndexController::class, 'index']);
$app->get('/subscription', [SubscriptionController::class, 'subscriptionForm'])->setName('subscriptionForm');
$app->post('/subscription', [SubscriptionController::class, 'subscribe'])->add(new ExampleMiddleware);
$app->addRoutingMiddleware();

// Swoole part.

```

```
44. $server_address = $_ENV['SERVER_ADDRESS'] ?? '127.0.0.1';
45. $server_port = $_ENV['SERVER_PORT'] ?? '9503';
46.
47. $server = new Server($server_address, $server_port);
48.
49. $server->set([
50.     'document_root' => __DIR__ . '/public',
51.     'enable_static_handler' => true,
52.     'static_handler_locations' => ['/imgs'],
53. ]);
54.
55. $server->on("start", function (Server $server) use ($server_address, $server_port) {
56.     echo "HTTP server available at http://" . $server_address . ":" . $server_port .
PHP_EOL;
57. });
58.
59. $server->on("request", function (Request $request, Response $response) use ($app,
$requestConverter) {
60.     $psr7Request = $requestConverter->createFromSwoole($request);
61.     $psr7Response = $app->handle($psr7Request);
62.     $converter = new SwooleResponseConverter($response);
63.     $converter->send($psr7Response);
64. });
65.
66. $server->on('close', function ($server) {
67.     echo "Connection closed.\n";
68. });
69.
70. $server->start();
```

Reference in the repo: https://phpa.me/jacked-php-chapter-4-http_server_6

Note that at the `/subscription` route (line 48), we are calling the method `->add(new ExampleMiddleware)`. This “add” method adds the middleware to the subscription route.

The middleware, following the expected behavior, needs to be invokable. For that, the implementation follows what is in Listing 4.10. If you were not to implement anything in this middleware, the only content at the `_invoke` method would be `return $handler->handle($request)` - then it would do nothing, pass the request to the next item in the request pipeline middleware. I added an example of how to handle some processing via middleware by adding validation to the email submitted with the Subscription Form:

```php
<?php

namespace App\Http\Middlewares;

use Exception;
use Psr\Http\Message\ResponseInterface;
use Psr\Http\Message\ServerRequestInterface as Request;
use Psr\Http\Server\RequestHandlerInterface as RequestHandler;
use Slim\Psr7\Response;

class ExampleMiddleware
{
    /**
     * @param  Request  $request PSR-7 request
     * @param  RequestHandler $handler PSR-15 request handler
     *
     * @return Response
     */
    public function __invoke(Request $request, RequestHandler $handler): ResponseInterface
    {
        global $app;

        try {
            // @throws Exception
            $this->validateEmail($request);
        } catch (Exception $e) {
            $response = new Response();
            $routeParser = $app->getRouteCollector()->getRouteParser();
            $url = $routeParser->urlFor('subscriptionForm', [], ['error' => $e->getMessage()]);
            return $response
                ->withHeader('Location', $url)
                ->withStatus(302);
        }

        return $handler->handle($request);
    }

    /**
     * @param Request $request
     *
     * @return void
     *
     * @throws Exception
     */
```

```
    private function validateEmail(Request $request): void
    {
        $inputData = $request->getParsedBody();

        if (!isset($inputData['email']) || empty($inputData['email'])) {
            throw new Exception('Email is a required field.');
        }

        if (!filter_var($inputData['email'], FILTER_VALIDATE_EMAIL)) {
            throw new Exception('Invalid email.');
        }
    }
}
```

Reference in the repo: https://phpa.me/jacked-php-chapter-4-ExampleMiddleware

At the Controller, we also added some changes. They are basically to handle the error message, as seen in Listing 4.11.

```
<?php

namespace App\Http\Controllers;

use App\Http\Controllers\Traits\HasServerParams;
use Psr\Http\Message\ServerRequestInterface;
use Psr\Http\Message\ResponseInterface;
use League\Plates\Engine;

class SubscriptionController
{
    use HasServerParams;

    public function subscriptionForm(ServerRequestInterface $request,
ResponseInterface $response)
    {
        $serverParams = $this->getServerParams($request);

        echo "Incoming connection time: " . date('Y-m-d H:i:s') . PHP_EOL;
        echo "Incoming connection uri: " . $serverParams['REQUEST_URI'] ?? '' .
PHP_EOL;

        $queryParams = $request->getQueryParams();

        $data = [
            'main_heading' => 'Subscription Page',
        ];
```

```
        if (isset($queryParams['error']) && !empty($queryParams['error'])) {
            $data['error'] = $queryParams['error'];
        }

        $templates = new Engine(ROOT_DIR . '/html');
        $html_content = $templates->render('sample5', $data);

        $response->getBody()->write($html_content);
        return $response->withStatus(200);
    }

    public function subscribe(ServerRequestInterface $request, ResponseInterface $response)
    {
        $serverParams = $this->getServerParams($request);

        $data = $request->getParsedBody();

        echo "Incoming connection time: " . date('Y-m-d H:i:s') . PHP_EOL;
        echo "Incoming connection uri: " . $serverParams['REQUEST_URI'] ?? '' . PHP_EOL;
        echo "Incoming connection data: " . json_encode($data) . PHP_EOL;

        $templates = new Engine(ROOT_DIR . '/html');
        $html_content = $templates->render('sample5-result', [
            'main_heading' => 'Subscription Page Result',
            'email' => $data['email'],
        ]);

        $response->getBody()->write($html_content);
        return $response->withStatus(200);
    }
}
```

Reference in the repo: https://phpa.me/jacked-php-chapter-4-SubscriptionController

With this in hand, errors will be shown as expected when invalid data is sent. Please refer to the complete example for the HTML at the end of this chapter. This is one of many ways of doing it; we'll see soon verify an alternative way of messaging users about procedure outcomes.

Listening to Multiple Ports - Let's use HTTPS

When using OpenSwoole to serve an HTTP server with the previous examples, one question might come to mind: is there a way to listen to multiple ports? The answer to that question is simple: yes.

> *You might be asking yourself why that would be needed. The most common example is when you have a website running on HTTPS. HTTPS uses port 443, but some connections might try to hit your server in port 80 (HTTP) first. From port 80, your server would have to redirect the visitor to port 443 - a common strategy to force visitors to use the secure protocol.*

The process is quite simple, and it is part of how the `OpenSwoole\Server` behaves, which is the class that is the parent class of the HTTP Server. It uses the listen' method (https://openswoole.com/docs/modules/swoole-server-listen) in an `OpenSwoole\Server` instance. This subject is covered by OpenSwoole's documentation on this page: https://openswoole.com/docs/modules/swoole-server/multiple-ports.

Step 1: Generate a certificate

To start building an example, let's first generate a certificate. If you are preparing an app on a server with static IP, you can count on some paid certificate or even use a free Let's Encrypt[9] one. Here, you have two alternatives, (1) you can generate a self-signed certificate using OpenSSL[10] tool; for that, you can follow this tutorial: https://savioresende.com/blog/creating-a-self-signed-ssl-certificate - it covers both, generating self-signed certificates and the usage of Mkcert[https://github.com/FiloSottile/mkcert] for valid local certificates. If you decide on the self-signed alternative, you might need to use the parameter `ssl_allow_self_signed` in the OpenSwoole Server settings (reference: https://openswoole.com/docs/modules/swoole-server/configuration#usage-and-ssl-protocols) - that will avoid errors while working on your local environment.

[9] https://letsencrypt.org/
[10] https://www.openssl.org/

Step 2: implement the multiple port listening

The second step is simply the code. In Listing 4.12, you'll see an example of a server listening to both ports 80 and 443:

```php
<?php

use OpenSwoole\Constant;
use OpenSwoole\Http\Server;
use OpenSwoole\Http\Request;
use OpenSwoole\Http\Response;
use OpenSwoole\Server\Port;

$server = new Server("0.0.0.0", 80);

/** @var Port $sslPort */
$sslPort = $server->listen("0.0.0.0", 443, Constant::SOCK_TCP | Constant::SSL);

$sslPort->set([
    'ssl_cert_file' => __DIR__ . '/certs/local.swooleexample.com.pem',
    'ssl_key_file' => __DIR__ . '/certs/local.swooleexample.com-key.pem',
    'ssl_allow_self_signed' => false, // <- this can be useful for development environment
    'open_http_protocol' => true,
]);

$sslPort->on("request", function (Request $request, Response $response) use ($sslPort) {
    $response->end(sprintf("<h1>Server listening to port: %s.</h1>", $sslPort->port));
});

$server->on("start", function (Server $server) use ($sslPort) {
    echo sprintf('Swoole http server is started at http://%s:%s and http://%s:%s', $server->host, $server->port, $sslPort->host, $sslPort->port), PHP_EOL;
});

$server->on("request", function (Request $request, Response $response) use ($server) {
    $response->end(sprintf("<h1>Server listening to port: %s.</h1>", $server->port));
});

$server->start();
```

Reference in the repo: https://phpa.me/jacked-php-chapter-4-http_server_7

Before being able to test this snippet in your environment, consider following the referred tutorial (https://savioresende.com/blog/creating-a-self-signed-ssl-certificate). There, the certificates are expected to be generated with the respective names (in the snippet, the domain is "local.swooleexample.com") in the directory `__DIR__ . '/certs/` as shown the line 16.

Notice that each extra port we need to listen to is an additional call to the `listen` method at the server instance. The output of that method is the object `OpenSwoole\Server\Port`. To customize each of those calls to `listen`, you can keep the output of that call and invoke the callbacks that need to be different from the main server. In this example, the main server listens to port 80, and the extra port listened to is port 443. The output of the listen call that adds port 443 to this server is the variable `$sslPort`. At this variable, we call the method "set" to specify some configurations to port 443. For example, we also give a different callback to the event request, giving a different output to it.

> **Important**: *Some systems might require* **extra authorization to use port 80**. *If so, and that is not possible, try using different ports for the sake of the test, such as 8000 for HTTP and 8443 for HTTPS (or even try starting the server as a root user if there are no concerns about that). Also, for the domain to work, you might need to customize the host file in your system by adding* `127.0.0.1 {your-domain}` *line. Different OSs have different places to find the "hosts" file. This file is more commonly located on Linux at* `/etc/hosts`.

This server will result in what can be seen in Figure 4.11 and Figure 4.12 in the Browser and Figures 4.13 for the Terminal output.

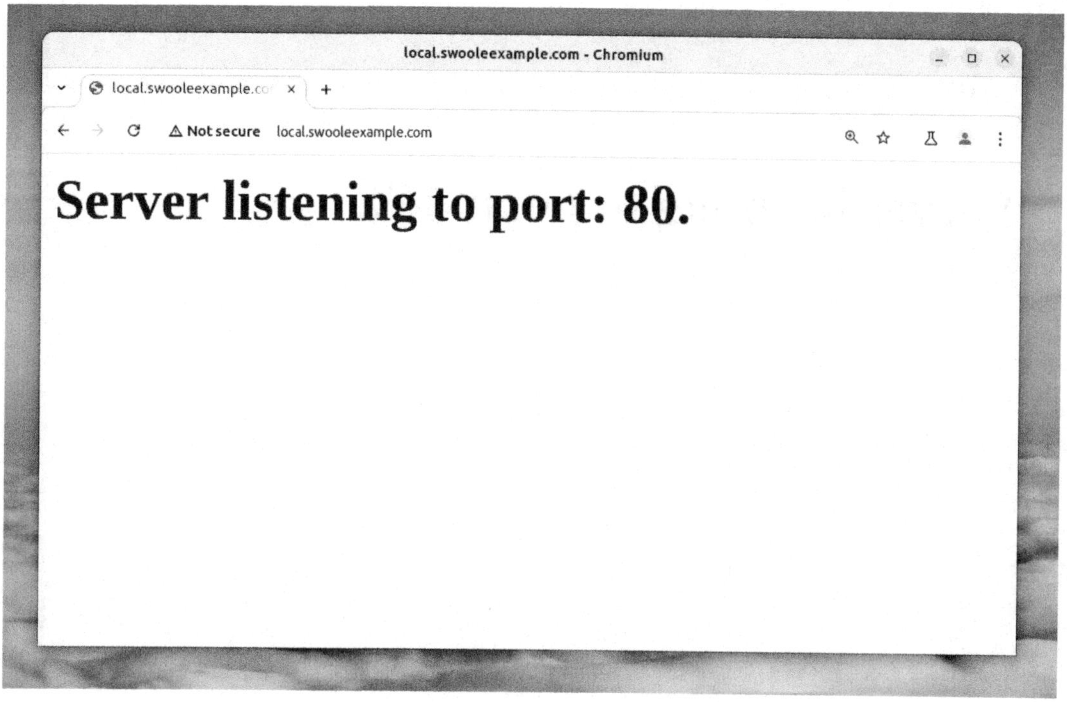

Figure 4.11 - Output of HTTP server listening to Port 80

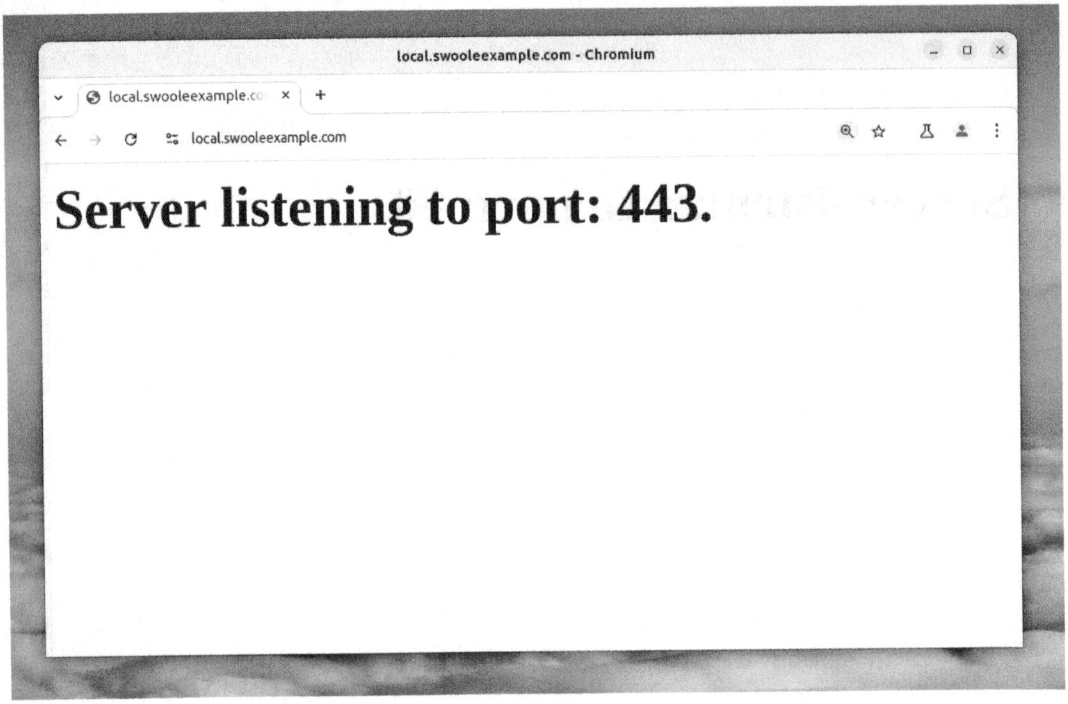

Figure 4.12 - Output of HTTPS server listening to Port 443

Figure 4.13 - Terminal output of server listening to Ports 80 and 443

Implementing a User Authorization

The way of implementing a User Authorization using an OpenSwoole Application like the one we've been building through this chapter is with Cookies. Using Cookies is as common as PHP Sessions, and sessions won't work correctly in a Coroutine server given the way it works: it is a shared environment through multiple requests concurrently. Because of that, the strategy will change a little.

Cookies will be used to keep, in the browser, the hash of what we will call "user session". The hash is the key for the record in the `OpenSwoole\Table`, where we keep information about the current context. This record will be helpful only while the server is on. When the server restarts, it won't exist anymore, and all sessions will expire even though the cookies stay in the browser. We won't need to worry about that because they become harmless when that happens.

The workflow of the authorization process goes like this:

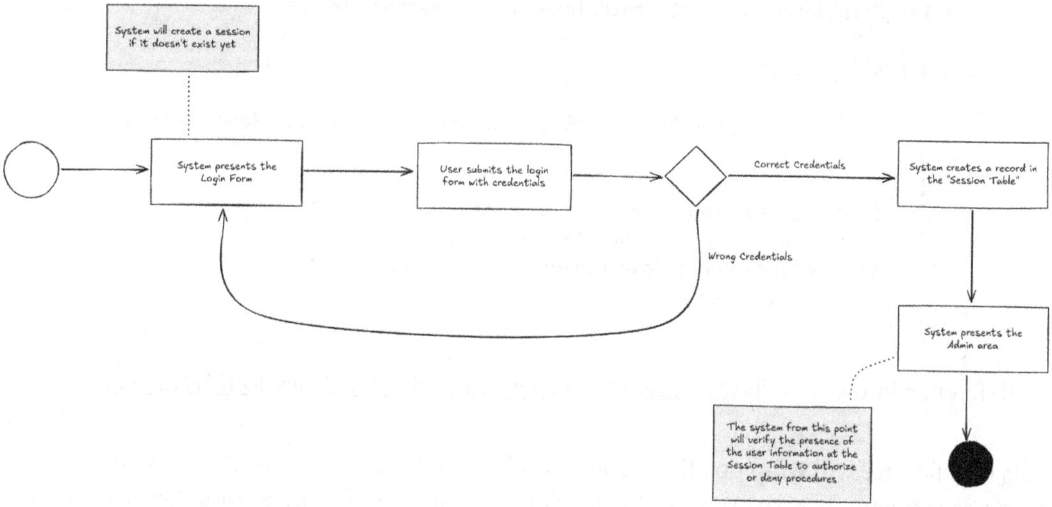

Figure 4.14: User Authorization workflow.

Step 1

First, we need a Session Middleware where we will prepare the cookies and keep the key to the session. The persistence strategy for this session key will be `OpenSwoole\Table`, which I'll refer to as Session Table. After any session verification, we will review the Session Table to verify if the current request is authorized.

Listing 4.13 shows the Session Middleware where the cookies keeping the session key are created if not existent:

```php
<?php

namespace MyCode\Http\Middlewares;

use Exception;
use MyCode\DB\User;
use MyCode\Services\Session;
use Psr\Http\Message\ServerRequestInterface;
use Psr\Http\Server\RequestHandlerInterface as RequestHandler;

class SessionMiddleware
{
    public function __invoke(ServerRequestInterface $request, RequestHandler $handler)
    {
        $request->session = Session::startSession($request);
        $response = $handler->handle($request);
        Session::addCookiesToResponse($request, $response);
        return $response;
    }
}
```

Reference in the repo: https://phpa.me/jacked-php-chapter-4-SessionMiddleware

This middleware will wrap up all our routes and create an identifier for that browser as soon as the page opens. The part responsible for adding that cookie is the Session Service added at the next step.

Step 2

Second, we create the Session service responsible for managing cookies. This service is a wrapper for the package in the background called Chocookies[11]. This package is a single file facilitator to add cookies at Psr7 request and response messages.

[11] https://github.com/lotharthesavior/chocookies

At the Listing 4.14 is this Service:

```php
<?php

namespace App\Services;

use Chocookies\Cookies;
use Ramsey\Uuid\Uuid;
use Psr\Http\Message\ResponseInterface;
use Psr\Http\Message\ServerRequestInterface as Request;

class Session
{
    public static function startSession(Request $request): array
    {
        $current_session = self::getCurrentSession($request);

        return $current_session;
    }

    public static function addCookiesToResponse(Request $request, ResponseInterface &$response): void
    {
        $data = $request->session;
        $session_data = SessionTable::getInstance()->get($data['id']);

        $cookies = [];

        foreach ($session_data as $key => $value) {
            if (!in_array($key, ['id'])) {
                continue;
            }
            $cookies[$key] = $session_data[$key];
        }
        Cookies::setCookie(
            $response,
            SessionTable::SESSION_KEY,
            self::encodeCookie($cookies)
        );
    }

    private static function getCurrentSession(Request $request): array
    {
        $session_table = SessionTable::getInstance();

        $session_data = Cookies::getCookie($request, SessionTable::SESSION_KEY);

```

```
        if (null !== $session_data) {
            $session_data = self::parseCookie($session_data);
        }
        if (empty($session_data)) {
            $session_data['id'] = Uuid::uuid4()->toString();
        }
        if (!$session_table->has($session_data['id'])) {
            $session_table->set($session_data['id'], $session_data);
        }
        $current_session = $session_table->get($session_data['id']);

        return $current_session ?? [];
    }

    private static function parseCookie(string $data)
    {
        $data = str_replace($_ENV['SESSION_KEY'], '', $data);
        return json_decode(base64_decode($data), true);
    }

    private static function encodeCookie(array $data): string
    {
        $data = json_encode($data);
        return $_ENV['SESSION_KEY'] . base64_encode($data);
    }
}
```

Listing 4.14: Service to manage cookies.

Reference in the repo: https://phpa.me/jacked-php-chapter-4-Session

This service has only two public methods: `startSession(Request $request)` and `addCookiesToResponse(Request $request, ResponseInterface &$response)`. The first creates a session for the current request or retrieves an existing one. The second is to add cookies to the response to create session awareness of the following requests. Both were called at the `SessionMiddleware`.

> **Notice**: *There is also a significant change: notice the usage of the* `SESSION_KEY` *environment key. That key is used in the* `encodeCookie` *method to increase the difficulty of cracking the data present there.*

Step 3

In the third step, we will create the Authorization middleware. This middleware manages what can be done and what cannot. Keep in mind that this is just a simple example, and any advanced implementation of such roles must go further than that.

This is presented at the Listing 4.15 Authorization middleware:

```php
<?php

namespace App\Http\Middlewares;

use App\Services\SessionTable;
use Nyholm\Psr7\Response;
use Psr\Http\Message\ServerRequestInterface;
use Psr\Http\Server\RequestHandlerInterface as RequestHandler;
use Slim\Routing\RouteContext;

class AuthorizationMiddleware
{
    public function __invoke(ServerRequestInterface $request, RequestHandler $handler)
    {
        $routeContext = RouteContext::fromRequest($request);
        $route = $routeContext->getRoute();
        $is_login_route = in_array($route->getName(), ['login', 'login-handler']);

        $session_table = SessionTable::getInstance();
        $session_data = $session_table->get($request->session['id']);

        if (!$is_login_route && !isset($session_data['user_id'])) {
            return (new Response)
                ->withHeader('Location', '/login')
                ->withStatus(302);
        }
        if ($is_login_route && isset($session_data['user_id'])) {
            return (new Response)
                ->withHeader('Location', '/admin')
                ->withStatus(302);
        }
        return $handler->handle($request);
    }
}
```

Reference in the repo: https://phpa.me/jacked-php-chapter-4-AuthorizationMiddleware

Step 4

In step 4, we will add the service responsible for keeping the ephemeral data about the session on the server side. This "service" could be a file, redis records, or even more advanced databases. Because of the temporary nature of this data and the advantage of keeping it fast and simple to manage, `OpenSwoole\Table` is an excellent alternative. To make it standard, the CacheInterface was chosen.

The Listing 4.16 shows this Service:

```
<?php

namespace App\Services;

use Carbon\Carbon;
use DateInterval;
use Psr\SimpleCache\CacheInterface;
use OpenSwoole\Table;

class SessionTable implements CacheInterface
{
    const SESSION_KEY = 'my-code-session';

    protected static ?SessionTable $instance = null;

    protected static Table $table;

    private function __construct()
    {
        self::$table = $this->createTable();
    }

    public static function getInstance(): SessionTable
    {
        if (self::$instance === null) {
            self::$instance = new SessionTable;
        }
        return self::$instance;
    }
    public static function destroyInstance(): void
    {
        self::$table->destroy();
        self::$instance = null;
    }

    protected function createTable(): Table
```

```
    {
        $table = new Table(1024);
        $table->column('data', Table::TYPE_STRING, 1000);
        $table->column('ttl', Table::TYPE_INT, 8);
        $table->create();
        return $table;
    }

    public static function getTable(): Table
    {
        return self::$table;
    }

    /**
     * Fetches a value from the cache.
     */
    public function get(string $key, mixed $default = null): mixed
    {
        if ($this->has($key)) {
            $value = self::$table->get($key);
            if (Carbon::now()->getTimestamp() < $value['ttl']) {
                return json_decode($value['data'], true);
            }
        }
        return $default;
    }

    /**
     * Persists data in the cache, uniquely referenced by a key with an optional expiration TTL time.
     */
    public function set(string $key, mixed $value, DateInterval|int $ttl = null): bool
    {
        return self::$table->set($key, [
            'data' => json_encode($value),
            'ttl' => $ttl ?? Carbon::now()->addHours(4)->getTimestamp(),
        ]);
    }

    /**
     * Delete an item from the cache with its unique key.
     */
    public function delete(string $key): bool
    {
        return self::$table->del($key);
    }
```

```

    /**
     * Wipes clean the entire cache's keys.
     */
    public function clear(): bool
    {
        $result = self::$table->destroy();
        $this->createTable();
        return $result;
    }

    /**
     * Obtains multiple cache items by their unique keys.
     */
    public function getMultiple(iterable $keys, $default = null): iterable
    {
        $data = [];
        foreach ($keys as $key) {
            $data[] = $this->get($key);
        }
        return !empty($data) ? $data : $default;
    }

    /**
     * Persists a set of key => value pairs in the cache, with an optional TTL.
     */
    public function setMultiple(iterable $values, $ttl = null): bool
    {
        $inserted = [];
        foreach ($values as $key => $value) {
            if (!$this->set($key, $value)) {
                $this->deleteMultiple($inserted);
                return false;
            }
            $inserted[] = $key;
        }
        return true;
    }

    /**
     * Deletes multiple cache items in a single operation.
     */
    public function deleteMultiple(iterable $keys): bool
    {
        foreach ($keys as $key) {
            if ($this->has($key)) {
                $this->delete($key);
```

```
            }
        }

        return true;
    }

    /**
     * Determines whether an item is present in the cache.
     */
    public function has(string $key): bool
    {
        return self::$table->exists($key);
    }
}
```

Listing 4.16: SessionTable, the cache where the session data is kept.

Reference in the repo: https://phpa.me/jacked-php-chapter-4-SessionTable

Step 5

Now is the time to prepare the controller. To keep it separate from the other examples of this chapter, we will put all the route endpoints of this example in one controller: `LoginController.php`.

Listing 4.17 shows the Login Controller:

```
<?php

namespace App\Http\Controllers;

use App\Services\SessionTable;
use League\Plates\Engine;
use Psr\Http\Message\RequestInterface;
use Psr\Http\Message\ResponseInterface;
use stdClass;

class LoginController
{
    private function getUsers(): array
    {
        $johnDoe = new stdClass;
        $johnDoe->id = 1;
        $johnDoe->name = 'John Doe';
        $johnDoe->email = 'john@doe.com';
```

```
        $johnDoe->password = password_hash('secret', PASSWORD_DEFAULT);
        return [$johnDoe];
    }

    public function home(RequestInterface $request, ResponseInterface $response)
    {
        $templates = new Engine(ROOT_DIR . '/html');
        $response->getBody()->write($templates->render('home'));
        return $response;
    }

    public function login(RequestInterface $request, ResponseInterface $response,
$args)
    {
        $templates = new Engine(ROOT_DIR . '/html');
        $response->getBody()->write($templates->render('login', ['message' => '']));
        return $response;
    }

    public function loginHandler(RequestInterface $request, ResponseInterface
$response, $args)
    {
        $data = $request->getParsedBody();

        // TODO: validation

        $user = current(array_filter($this->getUsers(), function($item) use ($data)
{
            return $item->email === $data['email'];
        }));

        // TODO: verify if the user was found

        if (!password_verify($data['password'], $user->password)) {
            return $response
                ->withHeader('Location', '/login?error=Failed to authenticate!')
                ->withStatus(302);
        }

        $session_table = SessionTable::getInstance();
        $session_table->set($request->session['id'], [
            'id' => $request->session['id'],
            'user_id' => $user->id,
        ]);

        return $response
            ->withHeader('Location', '/admin')
```

```
            ->withStatus(302);
    }

    public function logoutHandler(RequestInterface $request, ResponseInterface $response, $args)
    {
        // TODO: validation

        $session_table = SessionTable::getInstance();
        $session_table->set($request->session['id'], [
            'id' => $request->session['id'],
        ]);

        return $response
            ->withHeader('Location', '/login')
            ->withStatus(302);
    }

    public function admin(RequestInterface $request, ResponseInterface $response, $args)
    {
        $session_table = SessionTable::getInstance();
        $session_data = $session_table->get($request->session['id']);

        $user = current(array_filter($this->getUsers(), function($item) use ($session_data) {
            return $item->id === $session_data['user_id'];
        }));

        $templates = new Engine(ROOT_DIR . '/html');
        $response->getBody()->write($templates->render('admin', ['user_name' => $user->name]));
        return $response;
    }
}
```

Listing 4.17: LoginController responsible for the user authorization procedures.

Reference in the repo: https://phpa.me/jacked-php-chapter-4-LoginController

The private method `getUsers` is just a measure to simplify our way of keeping users for this example. It will serve a list of `stdClass` with one user. We also don't handle validations in this example for simplicity.

The `home` method is just the home index of the website for this example. Then we have the `login` procedure, where we present the login form. The `login handler` handles the form submission, authorizes the user, adds it to the session table, and redirects the user to the admin page. The `logoutHandler` remove the user from the session table. The `admin` is the protected screen.

Step 6

Now we go and prepare the server. The server here is the same version as some previous servers but with a different route structure. You can see it in Listing 4.18:

```php
<?php

const ROOT_DIR = __DIR__;

require __DIR__ . '/vendor/autoload.php';

use App\Http\Controllers\LoginController;
use App\Http\Middlewares\AuthorizationMiddleware;
use App\Http\Middlewares\SessionMiddleware;
use Dotenv\Dotenv;
use Ilex\SwoolePsr7\SwooleResponseConverter;
use Ilex\SwoolePsr7\SwooleServerRequestConverter;
use Nyholm\Psr7\Factory\Psr17Factory;
use Slim\App;
use Slim\Routing\RouteCollectorProxy;
use OpenSwoole\Http\Request;
use OpenSwoole\Http\Response;
use OpenSwoole\HTTP\Server;

// Load config.
$dotenv = Dotenv::createImmutable(__DIR__);
$dotenv->load();

// Section: Start Psr7 Converter.
$psr17Factory = new Psr17Factory();
$requestConverter = new SwooleServerRequestConverter(
    $psr17Factory,
    $psr17Factory,
    $psr17Factory,
    $psr17Factory
);

// Section: Start Request Handler (Slim).

$app = new App($psr17Factory);
```

```php
$app->group('', function (RouteCollectorProxy $group) {
    $group->get('/', [LoginController::class, 'home']);

    $group->group('', function (RouteCollectorProxy $group2) {
        $group2->get('/login', [LoginController::class, 'login'])->setName('login');
        $group2->post('/login', [LoginController::class, 'loginHandler'])->setName('login-handler');
        $group2->post('/logout', LoginController::class . ':logoutHandler')->setName('logout-handler');
        $group2->get('/admin', [LoginController::class, 'admin'])
            ->setName('admin');
    })->add(new AuthorizationMiddleware);

})->add(new SessionMiddleware);
$app->addRoutingMiddleware();

// Swoole part.

$server_address = $_ENV['SERVER_ADDRESS'] ?? '127.0.0.1';
$server_port = $_ENV['SERVER_PORT'] ?? '9503';

$server = new Server($server_address, $server_port);

$server->set([
    'document_root' => __DIR__ . '/public',
    'enable_static_handler' => true,
    'static_handler_locations' => ['/imgs', '/css'],
]);

$server->on("start", function (Server $server) use ($server_address, $server_port) {
    echo "HTTP server available at http://" . $server_address . ":" . $server_port . PHP_EOL;
});

$server->on("request", function (Request $request, Response $response) use ($app, $requestConverter) {
    $psr7Request = $requestConverter->createFromSwoole($request);
    $psr7Response = $app->handle($psr7Request);
    $converter = new SwooleResponseConverter($response);
    $converter->send($psr7Response);
});

$server->on('close', function ($server) {
    echo "Connection closed.\n";
});

$server->start();
```

Listing 4.18: Server example with User Authorization.

Reference in the repo: https://phpa.me/jacked-php-chapter-4-http_server_8

Step 7

Here we add the assets:

```
.erro-message {
    color: red;
    margin-bottom: 10px;
}

.form-row {
    margin-bottom: 10px;
}

.login-form-container {
    margin: 0 auto;
    width: 780px;
    padding: 0px 10px 20px 10px;
    border: 1px solid #000;
}

h1 a {
    text-decoration: none;
    color: #000;
}
```

Listing 4.19: CSS stylesheet.

Reference in the repo: https://phpa.me/jacked-php-chapter-4-style

```
<html>
<head>
    <title>Home Page</title>
    <link rel="icon" href="data:,"><!-- This avoids errors for favicon requests -->

    <link rel="stylesheet" href="/css/style.css"/>
</head>
<body>

<div class="login-form-container">
    <h1>Home</h1>

    <div><a href="/login">Login</a></div>
</div>

</body>
</html>
```

Listing 4.20: HTML home page.

Reference in the repo: https://phpa.me/jacked-php-chapter-4-home

```
<html>
<head>
    <title>Admin Page</title>
    <link rel="icon" href="data:,"><!-- This avoids errors for favicon requests -->

    <link rel="stylesheet" href="/css/style.css"/>
</head>
<body>

<div class="login-form-container">
    <h1>Hello <?php echo $user_name; ?></h1>

    <form action="/logout" method="POST" enctype="multipart/form-data"><input
type="submit" value="Logout"/></form>
</div>

</body>
</html>
```

Listing 4.21: HTML admin page.

Reference in the repo: https://phpa.me/jacked-php-chapter-4-admin

```
<html>
<head>
    <title>Login Page</title>
    <link rel="icon" href="data:,"><!-- This avoids errors for favicon requests -->

    <link rel="stylesheet" href="/css/style.css"/>
</head>
<body>

<div class="login-form-container">
    <h1><a href="/"><</a> Login Page</h1>

    <div class="erro-message"><?=$message?></div>

    <form method="POST" action="/login" enctype="multipart/form-data">
        <div class="form-row">
            <div><label for="email">Email</label></div>
            <div><input name="email" type="text"/></div>
        </div>

        <div class="form-row">
            <div><label for="email">Password</label></div>
            <div><input name="password" type="password"/></div>
        </div>

        <div><input name="submit" type="submit" value="Submit"/></div>
    </form>

</div>

</body>
</html>
```

Listing 4.22: HTML login page.

Reference in the repo: https://phpa.me/jacked-php-chapter-4-login

The outcome of this user authorization implementation are in Figure 4.15, 4.16, and 4.17:

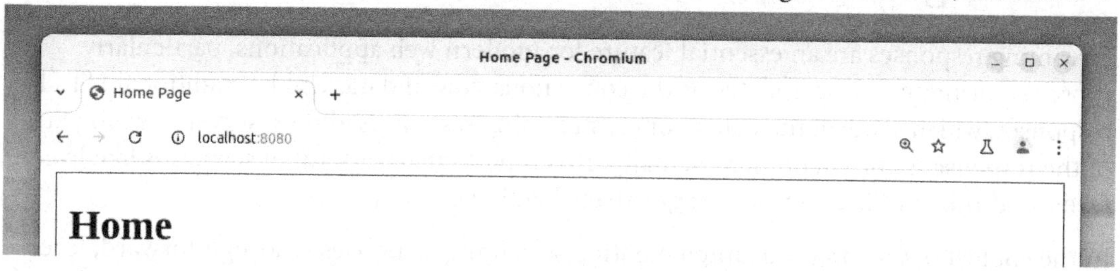

Figure 4.15: Home page.

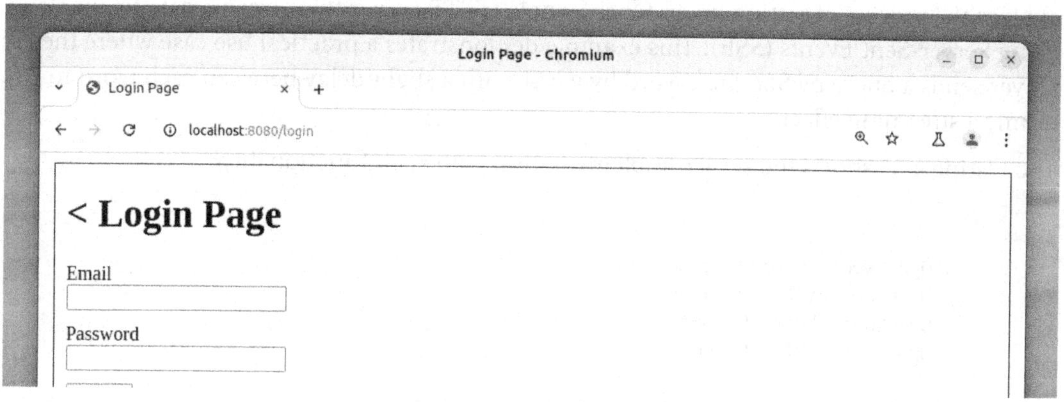

Figure 4.16: Login page.

With the mentioned example, after login with the user john@doe.com and password "secret", you'll get to the admin page:

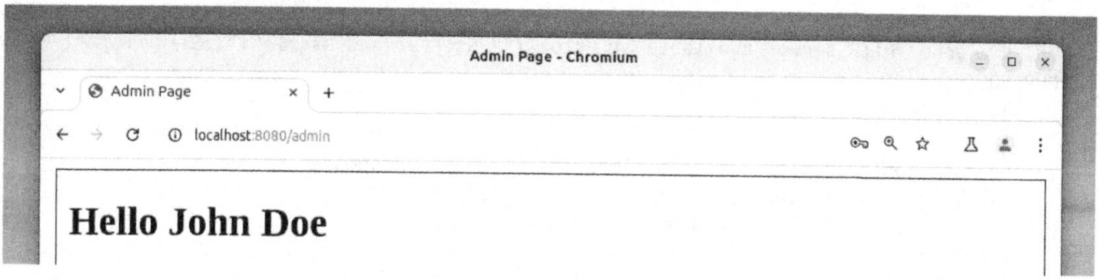

Figure 4.17: Admin page.

Streaming Responses

Streaming responses are an essential feature for modern web applications, particularly those requiring real-time updates or the continuous flow of data. Unlike traditional HTTP responses, which send all the data at once, streaming responses allow a server to send parts of the response to the client incrementally. This is particularly useful in scenarios like live feeds, real-time notifications, or progressively loading content.

In the context of OpenSwoole, implementing streaming responses is straightforward, leveraging its coroutine capabilities to manage asynchronous operations efficiently. Below, we explore the process of setting up an OpenSwoole HTTP server that streams data to clients using Server-Sent Events (SSE). This example demonstrates a practical use case where the server sends a quote by Socrates, word by word, with a slight delay between each word to mimic a streaming effect.

The Listing 4.23 shows the server implementation with such functionality:

```
<?php

use OpenSwoole\Coroutine;
use OpenSwoole\Http\Request;
use OpenSwoole\Http\Response;
use OpenSwoole\HTTP\Server;

$server_address = $_ENV['SERVER_ADDRESS'] ?? '127.0.0.1';
$server_port = $_ENV['SERVER_PORT'] ?? '9503';

$server = new Server($server_address, $server_port);

$server->on("start", function (Server $server) use ($server_address, $server_port) {
    echo "HTTP server available at http://". $server_address . ":". $server_port . PHP_EOL;
});

$server->on("request", function (Request $request, Response $response) {
  if ($request->server['request_uri'] === '/fe') {
        $html_content = <<<HTML
<!DOCTYPE html>
<html lang='en'>
<head>
    <meta charset="UTF-8">
  <meta name="viewport" content="width=device-width, initial-scale=1.0">
  <title>SSE Test</title>
</head>
<body>
```

```
<h1>Server-Sent Events Test</h1>

<div id="events">
    <strong>Streaming data: </strong>
        <p></p>
</div>

<script>
    const eventSource = new EventSource("/");

    eventSource.onmessage = function(event) {
                const eventContainer = document.getElementById("events");
                const paragraph = eventContainer.querySelector("p");
                if (event.data === "END") {
                        eventSource.close();
                        return;
                }
                paragraph.textContent += event.data + " ";
    };

    eventSource.onerror = function() {
                console.error("An error occurred with the SSE connection.");
        };
</script>
</body>
</html>
HTML;
        $response->header("Content-Type", "text/html");
        $response->end($html_content);
        return;
    }

    $response->header('Content-Type', 'text/event-stream');
    $response->header('Cache-Control', 'no-cache');
    $response->header('Connection', 'keep-alive');

    // write a Socrates quote
    $text = "Hello, I'm a server-sent event: 'The only true wisdom is in knowing you know nothing.' - Socrates END";

    $words = explode(' ', $text);

    foreach ($words as $word) {
        $response->write("data: {$word}\n\n");
        Coroutine::usleep(100000);
    }
    $response->end();
```

```php
});

$server->on('close', function ($server) {
    echo "Connection closed.\n";
});

$server->start();
```

Listing 4.23: Server Sent Event example.

Reference in the repo: https://phpa.me/jacked-php-chapter-4-http_server_9

The following are the parts that make it possible:

1. **Setting Headers:** The headers `Content-Type: text/event-stream`, `Cache-Control: no-cache`, and `Connection: keep-alive` are essential for Server-Sent Events (SSE). They ensure that the client remains connected and ready to receive continuous updates from the server.
2. **Creating the Message:** The message, a quote from Socrates, is split into individual words. It allows us to send each word separately, creating a streaming effect.
3. **Streaming the Data:** Using a coroutine, we send each word with a delay of 100 milliseconds (`Coroutine::usleep(100000)`). This delay simulates a real-time streaming experience. The `write` method sends data to the client incrementally, and the `end` method finalizes the response once all words have been sent.

To access this example just run it with `php http_server_9.php` and open the browser at the address `http://localhost:9503/fe` (this is the URI of the html part that then retrieves the SSE from the base endpoint). You will see the quote from Socrates being streamed word by word.

> *If you access `http://localhost:9503` (the base endpoint), it won't work properly in Firefox. While Chromium-based browsers handle it without issues, Firefox requires you to use the `/fe` endpoint to see it functioning correctly.*

Using OpenSwoole's coroutine capabilities ensures the server can handle other requests efficiently while streaming data, maintaining high performance and responsiveness.

Practical Considerations

When implementing streaming responses, several practical considerations must be addressed:

1. **Client-Side Handling:** Ensure that the client-side application is capable of handling SSE. It typically involves using JavaScript to listen for events, update the DOM, or perform other actions based on the received data.
2. **Error Handling:** Proper error-handling mechanisms should be in place to manage network issues, server errors, or unexpected client disconnections. It might include retry logic on the client side or graceful failure.
3. **Performance:** While streaming responses are powerful, they can be resource-intensive. Ensure the server and network infrastructure can handle the load, especially in high-traffic scenarios.

Streaming responses, particularly using SSE, provide an efficient way to deliver real-time data to clients. OpenSwoole's support for coroutines makes it well-suited for this task, allowing developers to build high-performance, scalable applications.

Benchmark

If you are curious about the benchmarks, at their website (https://openswoole.com/benchmark[12] , they also provide some so you can compare with other alternatives such as PHP-FPM with some webserver. On that website, they also mention the benchmark made by TechEmpower that compares OpenSwoole's performance with the rest of the solutions out there. At the time of this book edition, the results from that benchmark are shown in Figure 4.18. As seen, OpenSwoole stays above many other very popular technologies.

[12] https://openswoole.com/benchmark

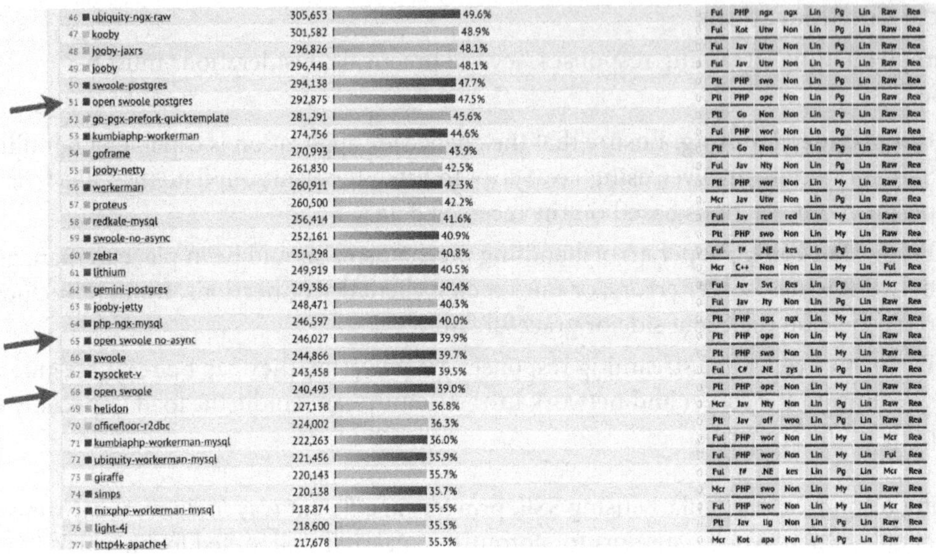

Figure 4.18: Benchmark comparing Swoole with other solutions

Reference: https://www.techempower.com/benchmarks/#section=data-r21

Conclusion

At this point, you have an excellent example of all the pieces needed to build functional HTTP servers from scratch using OpenSwoole with extra details to make your work professional. Always pay attention to the objects available within OpenSwoole and their interface so you use the best options at hand, such as the properties in the `Request` object.

Chapter 5

Setting up a WebSocket Server

Examples of this chapter:
https://phpa.me/jacked-php-chapter-5-examples

Let's create a WebSocket Server using PHP OpenSwoole and interact with it using a web page. This chapter provides the core principles for building real-time applications.

Here, we don't go through the same details as in Chapter 4, such as adding environment variables or adding SSL. Both processes are the same for WebSocket Servers within OpenSwoole, given that both are located in the abstraction from which WebSocket and HTTP implementations are based.

To begin with, we have to understand Sockets. According to Gay W.:

> *Sockets are like telephones in another way. To telephone someone, dial the telephone number of the party you want to contact. Sockets have network addresses instead of telephone numbers. By indicating the address of the remote socket, your program can establish a line of communication between your local socket and that remote endpoint.*
>
> *Gay, W. (2000). Linux Socket Programming. Que.*

When you start a Socket connection, messages can flow both ways. That is the main difference from a simple HTTP connection, which has the message flowing only in one direction. When you access a simple website that doesn't have WebSockets, the only way to get more information from the server is by making a new request to the server asking for it. In the WebSockets case, on the other hand, the server can push new data to the client when further information is available without that client making new requests.

As an example of one application that uses WebSockets, we have Slack, which keeps a very intensive message transit between clients and servers. Every time you send a message to another person there, the other person if connected, will receive a message from the server without making a new request for such - the message will come from the server to the client because the server knows how to connect each client. That happens because the server knows a specific WebSocket connection belongs to a particular user. When that user receives a message, the server dispatches a message to that connection. It would be something like in Figure 5.1:

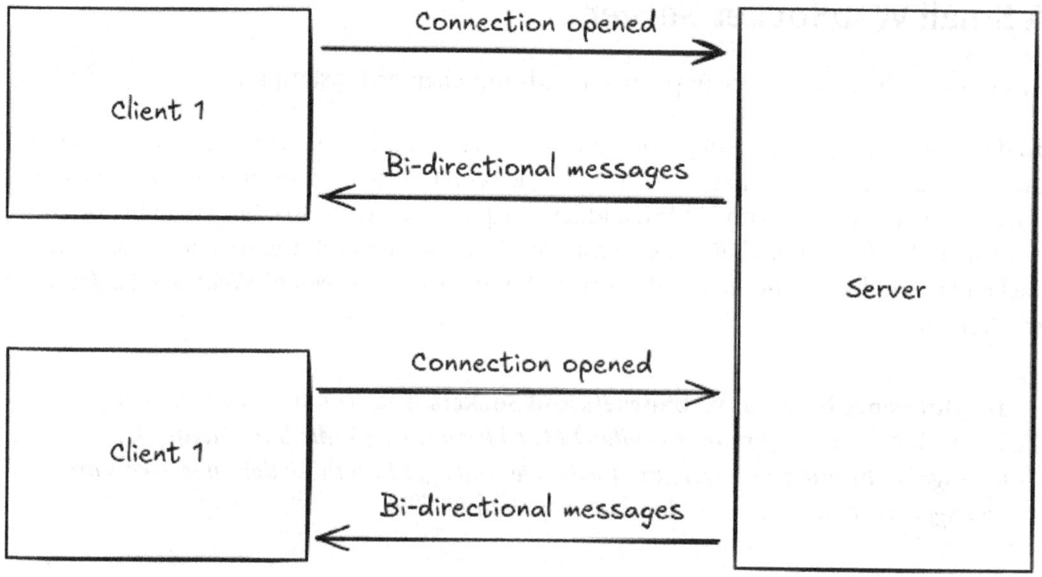

Figure 5.1: Image showing how Clients interact with Servers via WebSockets connections.

Many algorithms allow compelling functionalities on top of WebSockets. One of them is real-time collaboration. This powers many functionalities on demand, such as real-time editors like Google Docs. They use a technology called Operational Transformation[1]. A type of open source of it is called ShareDB[2], a JS project where you get the same benefits.

Returning to PHP OpenSwoole, see this example in the next section.

> **Note**: *It is possible to serve WebSocket and HTTP connections with the same server using OpenSwoole. We will gradually get there throughout this chapter. Until then, some examples expect you to use the PHP builtin server (`php -S 0.0.0.0:8000`).*

[1] https://javascript-operational-transformation.readthedocs.io/en/latest/what-is-ot.html
[2] https://share.github.io/sharedb/

A Small WebSocket Server

Reference in the repo: https://phpa.me/jacked-php-chapter-5-example1

To develop a WebSocket Service, you'll need the Server and the Client. The client, usually the Front End, is the part that interacts with the server. If that is a Front End, that goes in the browser and is built with HTML and Javascript, but there is also the possibility of having it made in the Back End. That is less common. When we are building socket services for backend technologies, the standard way is to build Sockets instead of WebSockets. Yes, they are different.

> **The difference between WebSockets and Sockets**: *both run over TCP/IP, but WebSockets run on a protocol similar to HTTP, requiring some bureaucracy for messages to be processed back and forth. We won't get into those details. Sockets are more generic and require less bureaucracy than HTTP.*

As in the HTTP Server, the WebSocket Server also happens via events. That said, it would look like this in Listing 5.1:

```php
<?php

use OpenSwoole\Http\Response;
use OpenSwoole\Websocket\Server;
use OpenSwoole\Http\Request;
use OpenSwoole\WebSocket\Frame;

$server = new Server("0.0.0.0", 9501);

$server->on('start', function (Server $server) {
    echo 'OpenSwoole WebSocket Server is started at http://127.0.0.1:9501' . PHP_EOL;
});

$server->on('open', function(Server $server, Request $request) {
    echo 'Connection open: ' . $request->fd . PHP_EOL;
});

$server->on("request", function (Request $request, Response $response) {
    echo "Incoming connection time: " . date('Y-m-d H:i:s') . PHP_EOL;
    echo "Incoming connection uri: " . $request->server['request_uri'] . PHP_EOL;

    $html_content = file_get_contents(__DIR__ . '/index.html');

    $response->header("Content-Type", "text/html");
    $response->header("Charset", "UTF-8");
    $response->end($html_content);
});

$server->on('message', function(Server $server, Frame $frame) {
    echo 'Received message: ' . $frame->data . PHP_EOL;
    $server->push($frame->fd, 'Your message: ' . $frame->data);
});

$server->on('close', function(Server $server, $fd) {
    echo 'connection close: ' . $fd . PHP_EOL;
});

$server->start();
```

Reference in the repo: https://phpa.me/jacked-php-chapter-5-websocket-server

The WebSocket server is similar to the HTTP server. It inherits the same interface: `OpenSwoole\Server` (https://openswoole.com/docs/modules/swoole-server-doc), and one extends from the other. It observes more events, though.

This would be a sample of a Frontend to interact with this server (Listing 5.2):

```
<!DOCTYPE html>
<html>
<head>
    <title>Sample Socket Client UI</title>
</head>
<body>
    <div class="container">
        <h1>WebSocket Client</h1>
        <form id="message-form">
            <div>
                <textarea id="message-box"></textarea>
            </div>
            <div>
                <input type="submit" />
            </div>
        </form>
        <hr/>
        <ul id="output"></ul>
    </div>
    <script type="text/javascript">

        (function() {

            var app = {
                ws: null,

                config: {
                    uri: 'ws://127.0.0.1',
                    port: 9501,
                },

                init: () => {
                    app.connectToServer();
                    app.listenEvents();
                },

                listenEvents: () => {
                    document.getElementById('message-form').addEventListener("submit", app.handleFormSubmit, false);
                },
```

```

                connectToServer: () => {
                    var wsServer = app.config.uri + ':' + app.config.port;
                    app.ws = new WebSocket(wsServer);

                    app.ws.onopen = function (evt) {
                        console.log("Connected to WebSocket server.");
                    };

                    app.ws.onclose = function (evt) {
                        console.log("Disconnected");
                    };

                    app.ws.onmessage = function (evt) {
                        console.log('Retrieved data from server: ' + evt.data);
                        app.handleIncomingMessage(evt.data);
                    };

                    app.ws.onerror = function (evt, e) {
                        console.log('Error occured: ' + evt.data);
                    };
                },

                /**
                 * @param {Event} e
                 */
                handleFormSubmit: (e) => {
                    e.preventDefault();
                    app.ws.send(document.getElementById('message-box').value);
                },

                /**
                 * @param {String} data
                 */
                handleIncomingMessage: (data) => {
                    let input = document.createElement("li");
                    input.innerText = data;
                    document.getElementById('output').appendChild(input);
                },
            };
            app.init();
        })();
    </script>
</body>
</html>
```

Reference in the repo: https://phpa.me/jacked-php-chapter-5-index

At this client, what is basically happening is that at the load of the page, the `app` object begins with the `init` method. There, we start a WebSocket[3] instance (`app.startServer();`) to connect to the backend WebSocket server, and also start to listen DOM events[4] (`app.listenEvents();`) to manage the process of interaction.

This is how it looks like in the Command line when started (Figure 5.2):

Figure 5.2: WebSocket server running on Command-Line.

This is how it will look in the browser (Figure 5.3):

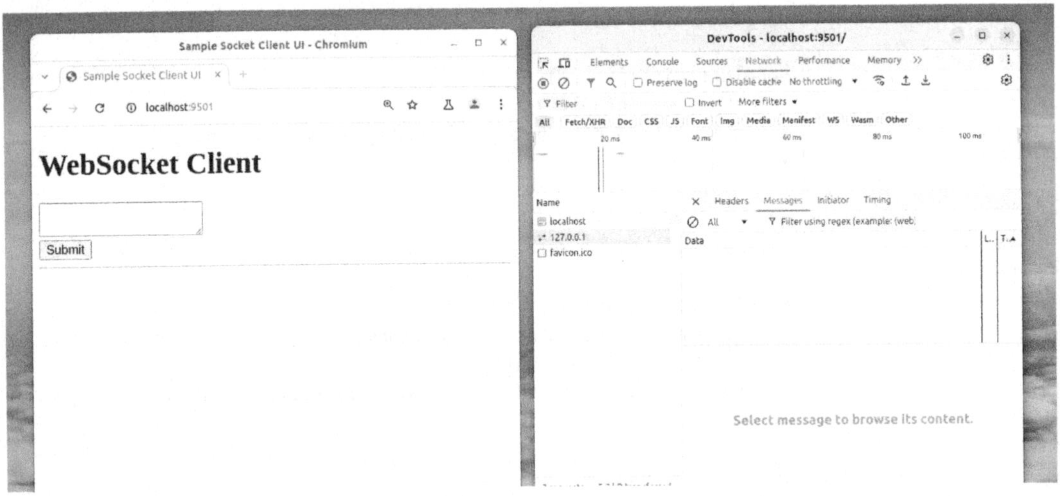

Figure 5.3: WebSocket Client UI.

---

[3] https://developer.mozilla.org/en-US/docs/Web/API/WebSocket
[4] https://developer.mozilla.org/en-US/docs/Web/API/Document_Object_Model/Events

As soon as you fill in the text area and submit the form, this is how they will look like (Figure 5.4 and Figure 5.5):

Figure 5.4: WebSocket Server after the first message.

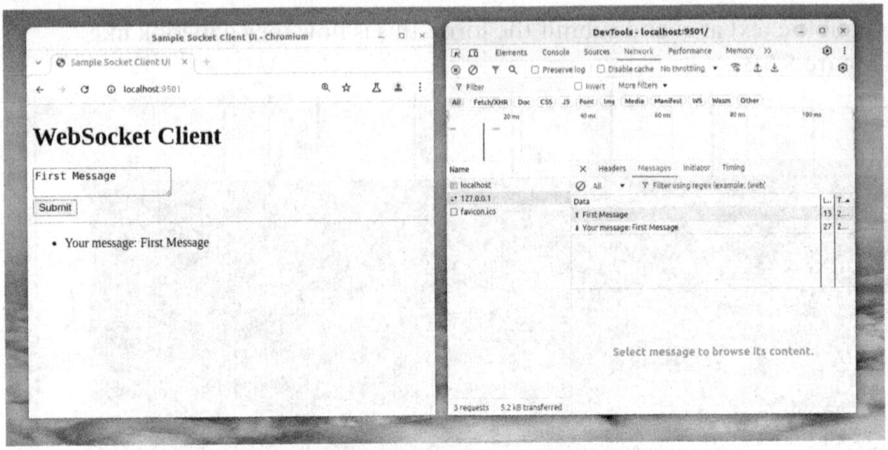

Figure 5.5: WebSocket Client UI after the first message.

This is a process of sending a message to the server, and the server sends a message back to the connection that sent the initial message. The WebSocket server knows the client by the File Descriptor (in the source code, this is, at the `open` event, the `$request->fd`, at the `message` event, the `$frame->fd`, and at the `close` event the `$fd`). We can understand "fd" as the id of the connection. It is the File Descriptor. That is a standard tool on Unix systems.

> *According to Michael Kerrisk (2010), "All system calls for performing I/O refer to open files using a file descriptor, a (usually small) nonnegative integer. File descriptors refer to all types of open files, including pipes, FIFOs, sockets, terminals, devices, and regular files. Each process has its own set of file descriptors." (p.69)*

A WebSocket Server for Multiple Clients

Reference in the repo: https://phpa.me/jacked-php-chapter-5-example2

The *FD* (File Descriptor) is the file on Linux used for the connection. That is how the server knows which client to send a message to. It identifies the connection. That is very useful when we want to keep a real-time interaction. As can be seen, by having the server aware of how to send a message to the client, the client doesn't need to make another request before getting any new data. The server can have more than one client connected. When that happens, the server will have an FD for each client connected; that way, it becomes possible to send messages to each connection independently. That is useful for applications such as chat or real-time notification systems. In a chat application, when a user sends a message to the server, that message gets broadcast to all other users connected to the same server. That can be filtered depending on the requirements of that chat.

For our following example, visit Figure 5.1. There you can see that there are two clients. There is a bidirectional message for each one of them. In that example, messages are being sent back and forth. When we receive a message from the first client, we will broadcast that message to all other connected clients. Once that happens, we can later distribute this message according to other conditions, such as the conversation that a given client participates in or something else. For the sake of simplicity, let's distribute to all connected clients.

To know the user for each connection, we will use **OpenSwoole Table**. OpenSwoole Table is a mechanism to share global data across multiple worker processes; in other words, this will make available this data in the global context of your application, and because OpenSwoole stays in memory, you will be able to access this data as long as your application doesn't get stopped or restarted. For that, Listing 5.3 shows how to use it. For further information on how OpenSwoole Table works, visit its documentation here: https://openswoole.com/docs/modules/swoole-table.

> **Important**: *let's consider the importance of OpenSwoole Table here. It happens that OpenSwoole is a Reactor-like server and starts multiple workers to handle the numerous incoming connections. Because of that, if you use something different from OpenSwoole Table, Redis, or some fast storage to handle the data from multiple workers, you might try to retrieve unavailable data when you need it. It happens that workers have process isolation.*

```php
<?php

use OpenSwoole\Table;

return function(): Table {
    $table = new Table(1024, 1);
    $table->column('id', Table::TYPE_INT);
    $table->column('name', Table::TYPE_STRING, 64);
    $table->create();
    return $table;
};
```

Reference in the repo: https://phpa.me/jacked-php-chapter-5-user-table

```php
<?php

use OpenSwoole\Websocket\Server;
use OpenSwoole\Http\Request;
use OpenSwoole\WebSocket\Frame;

$server = new Server("0.0.0.0", 9501);
$server->table = (require __DIR__ . DIRECTORY_SEPARATOR . 'user-table.php')();

$server->on("start", function (Server $server) {
   echo 'OpenSwoole WebSocket Server is started at http://127.0.0.1:9501' . PHP_EOL;
});

$server->on('open', function(Server $server, Request $request) {
    if (!isset($request->server['query_string'])) {
        $server->disconnect($request->fd, 401, 'Inform name for this connection.');
        return;
    }

    parse_str($request->server['query_string'], $parsed_query);
    $server->table->set($request->fd, ['id' => $request->fd, 'name' => $parsed_query['name']]);
    echo 'Connection open: ' . $request->fd . PHP_EOL;
});

$server->on('message', function(Server $server, Frame $frame) {
    $user_name = $server->table->get($frame->fd, 'name');

    echo 'Received message (' . $user_name . '): ' . $frame->data . PHP_EOL;
    $connections = $server->connection_list(0);
    foreach ($connections as $fd) {
        if ($frame->fd === $fd) {
            $server->push($fd, 'My message: ' . $frame->data);
        } else {
            $server->push($fd, $user_name . '\'s message: ' . $frame->data);
        }
    }
});

$server->on('close', function(Server $server, $fd) {
    echo 'Connection close: ' . $fd . PHP_EOL;
    $server->user_table->del($fd);
});

$server->start();
```

Reference in the repo: https://phpa.me/jacked-php-chapter-5-web-socket

```
<!DOCTYPE html>
<html>
<head>
    <title>Sample Socket Client UI</title>
</head>
<body>

    <div class="container">

        <h1>WebSocket Client <span id="user_name"></span></h1>

        <form id="message-form">
            <div>
                <textarea id="message-box"></textarea>
            </div>
            <div>
                <input type="submit" />
            </div>
        </form>

        <hr/>

        <ul id="output"></ul>

    </div>

    <script type="text/javascript">

        // string generator.
        const num = 8;
        const randomNameGenerator = num => {
            let res = '';
            for(let i = 0; i < num; i++){
                const random = Math.floor(Math.random() * 27);
                res += String.fromCharCode(97 + random);
            };
            return res;
        };

        (function() {

            /**
             * App State.
             */
            var state = {
                user_name: null,
            };
```

```

            /**
             * App Events.
             */
            var events = {
                SET_USER_NAME: 'set_user_name',
            };

            /**
             * App Actions.
             */
            var actions = {
                set_user_name: (name) => {
                    state.user_name = name;
                    document.dispatchEvent(new CustomEvent(events.SET_USER_NAME, {
                        detail: {user_name: name},
                    }));
                },
            };

            /**
             * App Core.
             */
            var app = {
                ws: null,

                config: {
                    uri: 'ws://127.0.0.1',
                    port: 9501,
                },

                /**
                 *
                 */
                init: () => {
                    app.listenEvents();
                    app.connectToServer();
                },

                /**
                 *
                 */
                listenEvents: () => {
                    document.getElementById('message-form').
addEventListener('submit', app.handleFormSubmit, false);
                    document.addEventListener(events.SET_USER_NAME, app.setUserName,
false)
```

```
            },

            /**
             *
             */
            connectToServer: () => {
                let name = prompt('Who are you?', randomNameGenerator(num));
                actions.set_user_name(name);

                if (app.ws !== null) {
                    if (!confirm('There is an active connection, do you wish to
close it?')) {
                        return;
                    } else {
                        app.ws.close();
                        app.ws = null;
                    }
                }

                var wsServer = app.config.uri
                    + ':'
                    + app.config.port
                    + '/?name='
                    + state.user_name;
                app.ws = new WebSocket(wsServer);

                app.ws.onopen = function (evt) {
                    console.log("Connected to WebSocket server.");
                };

                app.ws.onclose = function (evt) {
                    console.log("Disconnected");
                    app.ws = null;
                    console.log(evt.reason);
                };

                app.ws.onmessage = function (evt) {
                    console.log('Retrieved data from server: ' + evt.data);
                    app.handleIncomingMessage(evt.data);
                };

                app.ws.onerror = function (evt, e) {
                    console.log('Error occured: ' + evt.data);
                };
            },

            /**
```

```
                 * @param {Event} e
                 */
                handleFormSubmit: (e) => {
                    e.preventDefault();
                    app.ws.send(document.getElementById('message-box').value);
                },

                /**
                 * @param {String} data
                 */
                handleIncomingMessage: (data) => {
                    let input = document.createElement("li");
                    input.innerText = data;
                    document.getElementById('output').appendChild(input);
                },

                /**
                 * @param {Event} event
                 */
                setUserName: (event) => {
                    document.getElementById('user_name').innerText = '- ' + event.detail.user_name;
                },
            };

            app.init();
        })();

    </script>

</body>
</html>
```

Reference in the repo: https://phpa.me/jacked-php-chapter-5-example2-index

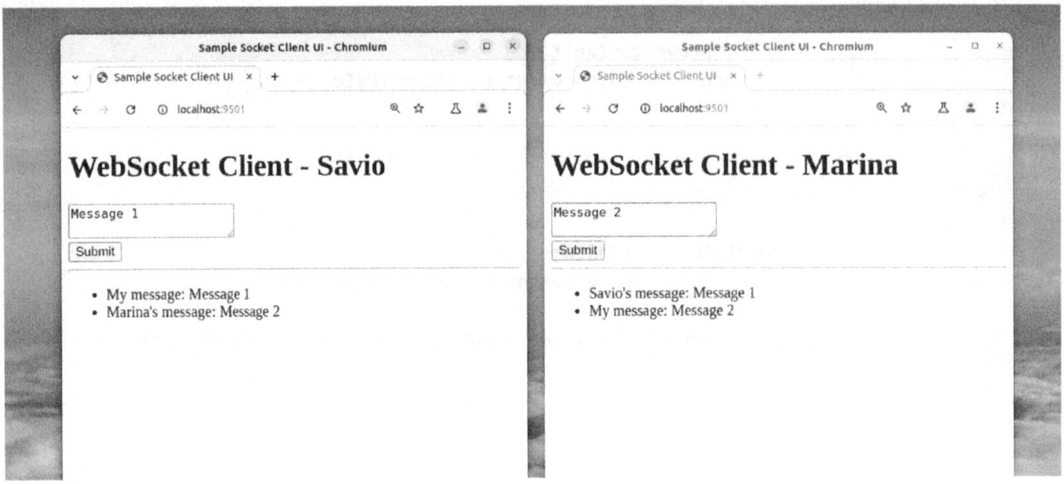

Figure 5.6: WebSocket Client UI with multiple Clients messaging each other.

Figure 5.7: Command line with server having multiple clients connections.

A WebSocket Server with message routing

Reference in the repo: https://phpa.me/jacked-php-chapter-5-example3

We discussed multiple clients' communication strategies using FDs (File Descriptors) in the previous section. Now, we will take a further step toward complexity: we will add extra actions that can be executed, keeping them abstracted and extensible within the application design.

In the previous example, we are handling the incoming request within the callback of the `message` event. That is not very extensible given that, as soon as your application starts handling more event patterns, you'll begin to have some hard decisions that will impact your application in the long run. In the given context, those decisions come to this: to accomplish different actions, we must decide on a pattern to "route" which specific function or class will handle each given "type" of incoming message from the client.

There is a PHP Package that can help us with that; it is called Socket Conveyor[5]. This package is an opinionated WebSocket subprotocol, just like Pusher or socketio. That means they decide on specific patterns of how messages must be structured to trigger specific actions. This package implements a few valuable features for projects with WebSockets, such as Channels, Fanouts, etc. That facilitates this step of the evolution of the application by standardizing all the motivations and decisions around message handling, which can easily take a lot of time for any project and become a rabbit hole.

Now, you can think of it as a Router for Socket Messages. The main idea is to be able to handle multiple procedures. That is entirely possible, but when doing so, we end up having much back and forth until we get to a good design that is testable and smooth. We can find examples of procedures within this package: it comes out of the box with some actions - the features it implements out-of-the-box. Between them, we have WebSocket Channels implementation (Figure 5.8). That means that, when connecting to the server, you can also say which channel you are connecting with. When that is specified, you'll be receiving messages and messaging only in that channel's context. Another important feature is the ability to broadcast messages across channels, including to connections that are not part of any channel (Figure 5.9). This means that even if you are inside a specific channel, any "fanout" event triggered on the server will reach your connection, no matter which connection sent the event. In this section, we'll focus on basic routing, which serves as the foundation for these advanced features.

---

[5] https://socketconveyor.com

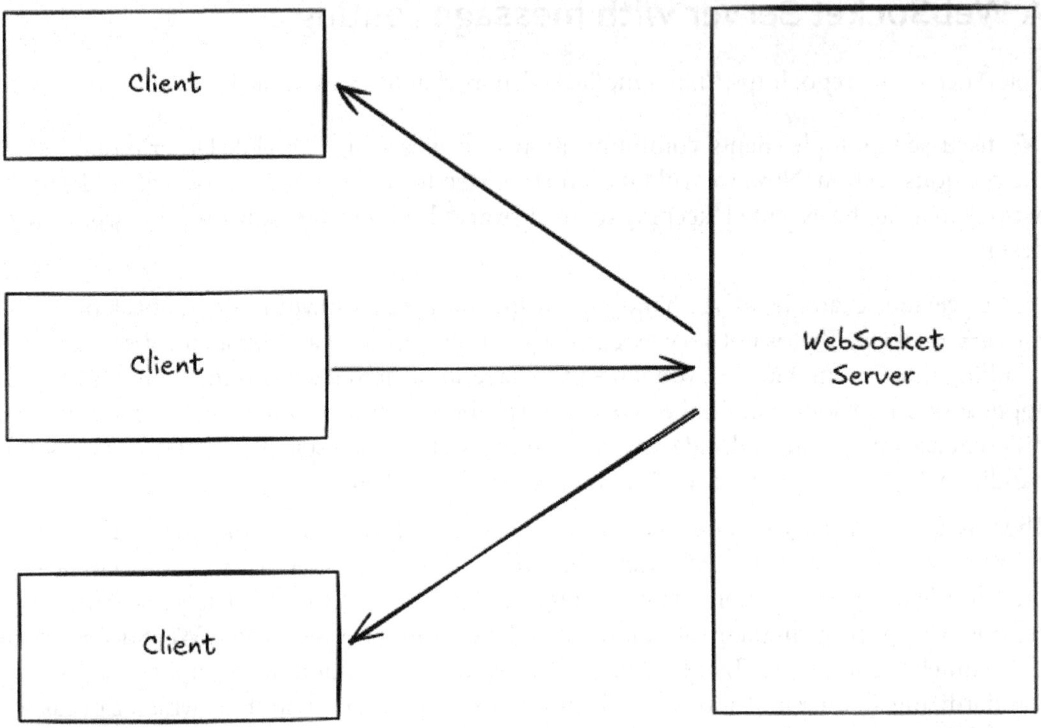

Figure 5.8: WebSocket Channels.

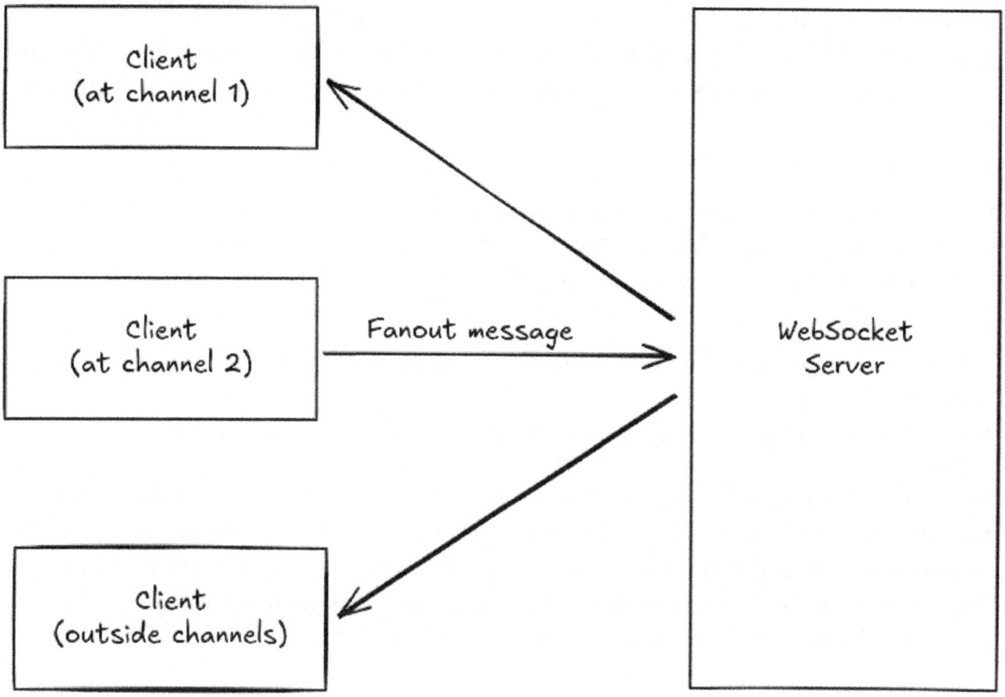

Figure 5.9: WebSocket Fanout.

To understand how that works, we will create different actions the clients can trigger via messages. For the sake of simplicity, we will keep the same example, and we will allow customers to delete their own messages sent to the list of messages.

We will also avoid some unnecessary concepts for this example, such as an Application Container (PSR-11[6] or Caching (PSR-6[7] .

[6] *https://www.php-fig.org/psr/psr-11/*
[7] *https://www.php-fig.org/psr/psr-6/*

To start that, we first need to install and implement our Socket Message Router. The package API consists of creating and specifying an Action in the Router. This Action will handle any incoming message at the `message` event of the given WebSocket Server. Instead of taking the incoming message ourselves, we will delegate it to the Router. The Router will analyze the message and invoke the expected Action.

You'll set up the actions once the package is installed in your project. To understand how to create an action, you can follow the documentation that, when this book was written, was located here: https://socketconveyor.com. For our requirements, we will have these 2 Actions:

- Add Action: responsible for adding the incoming messages to the message's list being displayed,
- Remove Action: responsible for removing messages from the message's list.

Another aspect that we need to consider before jumping into the implementation is that to have the messages sent between users able to be removed, you might want to add a piece of extra information, an identifier, to each message so that we make it removable by a more straightforward procedure. The ideal would be to organize the data in a Hash Table Data Structure[8] to refer to which message we want to remove quickly.

[8] https://en.wikipedia.org/wiki/Hash_table

Following, we have the examples at the Listings 5.6 and 5.7:

```php
<?php
namespace App\Actions;

use Conveyor\Actions\Abstractions\AbstractAction;

class AddMessage extends AbstractAction
{
    protected string $name = 'add-message';

    public function execute(array $data): mixed
    {
        $user_name = $this->server->user_table->get($this->fd, 'name');

        $next_id = $this->server->message_table->count() + 1;
        $this->server->message_table->set($next_id, [
            'fd' => $this->fd,
            'user_name' => $user_name,
            'message' => $data['message'],
        ]);

        foreach ($this->server->connections as $fd) {
            if ($this->fd === $fd) {
                $message = json_encode([
                    'id' => $next_id,
                    'action' => $this->name,
                    'message' => 'My message: ' . $data['message'],
                ]);
            } else {
                $message = json_encode([
                    'id' => $next_id,
                    'action' => $this->name,
                    'message' => $user_name . '\'s message: ' . $data['message'],
                ]);
            }
            $this->server->push($fd, $message);
        }
        return null;
    }
    public function validateData(array $data): void
    {
        // TODO: Implement validateData() method.
    }
}
```

Reference in the repo: https://phpa.me/jacked-php-chapter-5-addmessages

Here, we see partially the old code from the WebSocket server's callback `message` processing the incoming message; there are only a few differences related to the requirements of being able to delete messages afterward, which require some identifier. We have extra data, such as the method `$this->fd` used to get the connection file descriptor so you know which connection this handler executes the procedure for. Also, the `$this->server`, is used to make available for this action to execute the server's procedures, such as messaging something to a given connection FD. This is precisely what we use to send messages back and identify which user is sending the message. Notice that we are also sending with the message which action is happening. That is useful to identify the action to handle in the Front End.

The following is the other Action responsible for the message removal:

```php
<?php
namespace App\Actions;

use Conveyor\Actions\Abstractions\AbstractAction;
use Exception;

class DeleteMessage extends AbstractAction
{
    protected string $name = 'delete-message';

    public function execute(array $data): mixed
    {
        $user_name = $this->server->user_table->get($this->fd, 'name');

        $this->server->message_table->del($data['message_id']);

        foreach ($this->server->connections as $fd) {
            $this->server->push($fd, json_encode([
                'action' => $this->name,
                'delete_message_id' => $data['message_id'],
            ]));
        }

        return null;
    }
    public function validateData(array $data): void
    {
        // TODO: Implement validateData() method.
    }
}
```

Reference in the repo: https://phpa.me/jacked-php-chapter-5-deletemessage

There is a considerable change in the Front End of the code. Other than the procedures to handle the message deletion, some rearrangements are needed to make the code more understandable and maintainable. This is shown in the Listing 5.8. Pay special attention to the method `handleIncomingMessage`. That method handles any incoming message and decide how to proceed according to the action presented in it.

```
<!DOCTYPE html>
<html>
<head>
    <title>Sample Socket Client UI</title>
</head>
<body>

<div class="container">

    <h1>WebSocket Client <span id="user_name"></span></h1>

    <form id="message-form">
        <div>
            <textarea id="message-box"></textarea>
        </div>
        <div>
            <input type="submit" />
        </div>
    </form>

    <hr/>

    <ul id="output"></ul>

</div>

<script type="text/javascript">

    // string generator.
    const num = 8;
    const randomNameGenerator = num => {
        let res = '';
        for(let i = 0; i < num; i++){
            const random = Math.floor(Math.random() * 27);
            res += String.fromCharCode(97 + random);
        }
        return res;
    };

    (function() {
```

```

        /**
         * App State.
         */
        var state = {
            user_name: null,
        };

        /**
         * App Events.
         */
        var events = {
            SET_USER_NAME: 'set_user_name',
        };

        /**
         * App Actions.
         */
        var actions = {
            set_user_name: (name) => {
                state.user_name = name;
                document.dispatchEvent(new CustomEvent(events.SET_USER_NAME, {
                    detail: {user_name: name},
                }));
            },
        };

        /**
         * App Core.
         */
        var app = {
            ws: null,

            config: {
                uri: 'ws://127.0.0.1',
                port: 9501,
            },

            /**
             *
             */
            init: () => {
                app.listenEvents();
                app.connectToServer();
            },

            /**
```

```
         *
         */
        listenEvents: () => {
            document.getElementById('message-form').addEventListener('submit', app.handleFormSubmit, false);
            document.addEventListener(events.SET_USER_NAME,app.setUserName,false)
        },

        /**
         *
         */
        connectToServer: () => {
            let name = prompt('Who are you?', randomNameGenerator(num));
            actions.set_user_name(name);

            if (app.ws !== null) {
                if (!confirm('There is an active connection, close it?')) {
                    return;
                } else {
                    app.ws.close();
                    app.ws = null;
                }
            }

            var wsServer = app.config.uri
                + ':'
                + app.config.port
                + '/?name='
                + state.user_name;
            app.ws = new WebSocket(wsServer);

            app.ws.onopen = function (evt) {
                console.log("Connected to WebSocket server.");
            };

            app.ws.onclose = function (evt) {
                console.log("Disconnected");
                app.ws = null;
                console.log(evt.reason);
            };

            app.ws.onmessage = function (evt) {
                console.log('Retrieved data from server: ' + evt.data);
                app.handleIncomingMessage(evt.data);
            };

            app.ws.onerror = function (evt, e) {
```

```
                    console.log('Error occured: ' + evt.data);
                };
            },

            /**
             * @param {Event} e
             */
            handleFormSubmit: (e) => {
                e.preventDefault();
                app.ws.send(JSON.stringify({
                    action: 'add-message',
                    message: document.getElementById('message-box').value
                }));
            },

            removeMessage: (messageId) => {
                app.ws.send(JSON.stringify({
                    action: 'delete-message',
                    message_id: messageId
                }));
            },

            /**
             * @param {String} data
             */
            handleIncomingMessage: (data) => {
                const parsedData = JSON.parse(data);

                switch (parsedData.action) {

                    case "add-message":
                        let messageItem = app.createMessageItem(parsedData);
                        messageItem.appendChild(app.createDeleteMessageButton(parsedData));
                        document.getElementById('output').appendChild(messageItem);
                        break;

                    case "delete-message":
                        document.getElementById("message-" + parsedData.delete_message_id).remove();
                        break;

                    default:
                        console.log("Not recognized message received: " . data);
                        break;
                }
            },
```

```

            createMessageItem: (data) => {
                let input = document.createElement("li");
                input.id = "message-" + data.id;
                input.innerHTML = data.message;
                return input;
            },

            createDeleteMessageButton: (data) => {
                let button = document.createElement("a");

                button.title = "Remove message";
                button.innerHTML = "X";
                Object.assign(button.style, {
                    marginLeft: "10px",
                    color: "red",
                    fontWeight: "bold",
                    fontFamily: "Sans-Serif"
                });

                button.onclick = (e) => {
                    app.removeMessage(data.id);
                };

                return button;
            },


            /**
             * @param {Event} event
             */
            setUserName: (event) => {
                document.getElementById('user_name').innerText = '- ' + event.detail.user_name;
            },
        };

        app.init();
    })();

</script>

</body>
</html>
```

Reference in the repo: https://phpa.me/jacked-php-chapter-5-example3-index

The steps to verify this example are:

1. Install composer dependencies: `composer install`
2. Start the server: `php websocket-server.php`
3. Run php built-in server: `php -S localhost:8080`
4. Open the web page: `http://localhost:8080`

> *Notice that in this example we will make the HTTP server available using the built-in php server. In the next case, one of the improvements will be to serve the HTTP server from the same server.*

There are many possible improvement points, such as message validation improvement or some restrictions on who can execute actions, but this is enough for our goal here. Restriction improvement refers to analyzing whether a user can delete a message. More than hiding the button in the Front End for specific cases might be required. Let's explore that in the next section.

Adding a simple middleware strategy for socket messages

Reference in the repo: https://phpa.me/jacked-php-chapter-5-example4

To keep our connection secure, we must place some security verifications. According to the RFC 6455 (https://datatracker.ietf.org/doc/html/rfc6455), "The WebSocket server can use any client authentication mechanism available to a generic HTTP server, such as cookies, HTTP authentication, or TLS authentication". That said, the handshake event would be the best place if you want some authentication mechanism. Other than that, there are ways to identify users in later stages for many different purposes. An excellent reason for such that we have at hand here is to bind the connection (FD) to a user and, consequently, the ownership of the messages being sent. The simple step for that would be adding some Authorization at the Middleware stage of the message processing. Such verification might cost more time than affordable for the socket connection to be fast as it needs to be in real-time procedures, so we have to be thoughtful about how we are doing it, but at the end, we will have to measure the tradeoffs depending on the necessity of each project.

At this point, we mentioned two different ways to secure our OpenSwoole WebSocket server: (1) adding some authentication at the handshake event of the WebSocket server, (2) adding middlewares to the message processing so we can authorize or not specific actions.

After the last section, we still want to answer a question: which user can delete which message? With that in mind, let's see two different cases for Middleware for WebSocket connections. After answering that question, we will also see a simple procedure that can be added at the handshake event to authenticate users.

Case 1: Avoid users from deleting other user's messages.

This case is an authorization case. To prevent users who didn't create the message from deleting those messages, we can use our `OpenSwoole\Table` to match the incoming action to the owner of the message; if that is a match to the given message being deleted, we accept the action, if not, we deny. The first step is to add Middleware to our socket router. The Middleware needs to be a closure, or, as a class, to follow the interface `Conveyor\ActionMiddlewares\Interfaces\MiddlewareInterface` (a good reference of how this is expected to work; check the Pipeline[9] library from The PHP League[10] - this is because in Conveyor, middleware function as a pipeline. The official documentation for Conveyor's Middleware is located here: https://socketconveyor.com/docs/usage#case-4-use-middlewares.

Notice that this is not a middleware style that follows PSR-7 messages; this is a tunnel-style class in which, after executing a step, the previous step return is passed as the input of the next step. Following is an example of this Middleware verifying the incoming message for delete action. In this example, only the connection that sent the message can delete that message.

```php
<?php

namespace App\Middlewares;

use Conveyor\ActionMiddlewares\Interfaces\MiddlewareInterface;
use OpenSwoole\Table;
use Exception;

class DeleteMessageMiddleware implements MiddlewareInterface
{
    /**
     * @param mixed $payload
     *
     * @throws Exception
     */
    public function __invoke($payload): mixed
    {
        $data = $payload['data'];
        $fd = $payload['fd'];
        $server = $payload['server'];
        $messagesTable = $server->message_table;

        try {
            /** @throws Exception */
```

[9] https://pipeline.thephpleague.com/
[10] https://thephpleague.com/

```
            $this->isUserAllowedToDeleteMessage($fd, $data, $messagesTable);
        } catch (Exception $e) {
            $server->push($fd, json_encode([
                'action' => 'error',
                'message' => $e->getMessage(),
            ]));
            throw $e;
        }

        return $payload;
    }

    /**
     * @param int $fd
     * @param array $data
     * @param Table $messagesTable
     *
     * @throws Exception
     */
    public function isUserAllowedToDeleteMessage(int $fd, array $data, Table
$messagesTable): void
    {
        $message = $messagesTable->get($data['message_id']);

        if (!$message) {
            throw new Exception('Message not found in registers.');
        }

        if ($message['fd'] !== $fd) {
            throw new Exception('User not authorized to execute this procedure!');
        }
    }
}
```

Reference in the repo: https://phpa.me/jacked-php-chapter-5-middleware-deletemessage

```
<?php

use App\Actions\AddMessage;
use App\Actions\DeleteMessage;
use App\Middlewares\DeleteMessageMiddleware;
use Conveyor\Conveyor;
use OpenSwoole\Websocket\Server;
use OpenSwoole\Http\Request;
use OpenSwoole\WebSocket\Frame;

require __DIR__ . '/vendor/autoload.php';

$server = new Server("0.0.0.0", 9501);
$server->user_table = (require __DIR__ . DIRECTORY_SEPARATOR . 'user-table.php')();
$server->message_table = (require __DIR__ . DIRECTORY_SEPARATOR . 'message-table.php')();

$server->on("start", function (Server $server) {
    echo 'Swoole WebSocket Server is started at http://127.0.0.1:9501' . PHP_EOL;
});

$server->on('open', function(Server $server, Request $request) {
    if (!isset($request->server['query_string'])) {
        echo 'Closed due query string!' . PHP_EOL;
        $server->disconnect($request->fd, 401, 'Please, inform your name for this connection.');
        return;
    }

    parse_str($request->server['query_string'], $parsed_query);
    $server->user_table->set($request->fd, [
        'id' => $request->fd,
        'name' => $parsed_query['name'],
    ]);

    echo 'Connection open: ' . $request->fd . PHP_EOL;
});

$server->on('message', function(Server $server, Frame $frame) {
    $user_name = $server->user_table->get($frame->fd, 'name');

    echo 'Received message (' . $user_name . '): ' . $frame->data . PHP_EOL;

    $addMessage = new AddMessage;
    $deleteMessage = new DeleteMessage;

    Conveyor::init()
```

```
        ->server($server)
        ->fd($frame->fd)
        ->persistence()
        ->addActions([$addMessage, $deleteMessage])
        ->addMiddlewareToAction($deleteMessage->getName(), new
DeleteMessageMiddleware)
        ->run($frame->data);
});

$server->on('close', function(Server $server, $fd) {
    echo 'Connection close: ' . $fd . PHP_EOL;
    $server->user_table->del($fd);
});

$server->start();
```

Reference in the repo: https://phpa.me/jacked-php-chapter-5-example4-websocket-server

Important aspects to notice in this example are the information available at the Middleware so that the class was able to properly decide whether to allow a specific procedure. Middlewares in Conveyor will receive (at the version available at the moment this book was written):

- **data**: the OpenSwoole WebSocket parameter at the "message" event (`$frame->data`),
- **fd**: the connection FD,
- **server**: the OpenSwoole WebSocket Server instance,
- **user**: This was not used here, but if the user is identified by a Conveyor feature, the user reference will come here. To know more, visit https://socketconveyor.com/documentation/available-actions/#associate-user-to-fd.

The steps to verify this example are:

1. Install composer dependencies: `composer install`
2. Start the server: `php websocket-server.php`
3. Run php built-in server: `php -S localhost:8080`
4. Open the web page: `http://localhost:8080`

> *Notice that in this example we will make the HTTP server available using the built-in php server. In the next case, one of the improvements will be to serve the HTTP server from the same server.*

Case 2: Authentication at the handshake

Reference in the repo: https://phpa.me/jacked-php-chapter-5-example5

A good reference for security when it comes to the web is OWASP[11]. They talk about WebSocket connections in this cheat sheet series: https://cheatsheetseries.owasp.org/cheat-sheets/HTML5_Security_Cheat_Sheet.html#websockets. According to this document, verifying the "Origin" header at the connection is a good strategy. That can happen with a header parameter verification. Here, we won't go over this verification as the origin verification might simply be verifying some headers available at the request object. Instead, we will review more relevant strategies for connections between the server and browsers.

These verifications, when it comes to OpenSwoole, happen at the handshake. Initially, at that event, we will verify if the connection is coming from a proper WebSocket client; after that, we will verify a token that will authenticate the user. These will be the two steps to verify a proper connection from a user authorized to access this server.

Also, in this new example, we added the `request` event to our server so that we can serve our HTTP connection from within the same server.

Let's review what this new example will be doing step by step (including the cumulative features added from our previous example in Case 1):

The user will only be able to connect with a token. Each token belongs to a user, so we can identify that user using that token on the server side. Once the user connects to the HTTP request opening the web page with that token, the app will use a "single-use token" and apply it to the HTML so the web page can connect to the WebSocket server. This single-use token, as the name suggests, is only usable once. (In this example, you won't be able to connect again with the same token if you restart the web page. You can restart the server to be able to test again since the usage count is kept in the hard-coded array `$users`). We will share the user name retrieved from the user info based on the token with the client, so the client can display the user name. Users can delete messages for (not from) all connected users. That means that whenever they decide to delete their messages, they will also delete the messages for everybody else. Users won't be able to delete messages that belong to other users - only theirs.

---

[11] https://owasp.org/

Following is the example at Listing 5.11:

```
<?php

use App\Actions\AddMessage;
use App\Actions\DeleteMessage;
use App\Middlewares\DeleteMessageMiddleware;
use Conveyor\Conveyor;
use OpenSwoole\Http\Response;
use OpenSwoole\Websocket\Server;
use OpenSwoole\Http\Request;
use OpenSwoole\WebSocket\Frame;

require __DIR__ . '/vendor/autoload.php';

$host = '0.0.0.0';
$port = 9501;

$server = new Server($host, $port);
$server->user_table = (require __DIR__ . DIRECTORY_SEPARATOR . 'user-table.php')();
$server->message_table = (require __DIR__ . DIRECTORY_SEPARATOR . 'message-table.php')();

$users = [
    1 => [
        'name' => 'John Doe',
        'token' => '123456', // http token
        'token2' => 'extra123456', // ws token (single use)
        'token2_used' => false,
    ],
    2 => [
        'name' => 'Jane Doe',
        'token' => '7891011', // http token
        'token2' => 'extra7891011', // ws token (single use)
        'token2_used' => false,
    ],
];

/**
 * @param array<array-key, array{id:int,name:string,token:string,token2:string,token2_used:bool}> $users
 * @param string $token
 * @return ?array{id:int,name:string,token:string,token2:string,token2_used:bool}
 */
function getUserByToken(array $users, string $token, bool $singleUse = false): ?int {
    foreach ($users as $key => $user) {
```

```
        if (!$singleUse && $user['token'] === $token) {
            return $key;
        } elseif ($singleUse && $user['token2'] === $token && !$user['token2_used'])
{
            return $key;
        }
    }

    return null;
}

function processSecWebSocketKey(Request $request): array {
    $secWebSocketKey = $request->header['sec-websocket-key'];
    $patten = '#^[+/0-9A-Za-z]{21}[AQgw]==$#';

    if (
        0 === preg_match($patten, $secWebSocketKey)
        || 16 !== strlen(base64_decode($secWebSocketKey))
    ) {
        throw new Exception('Invalid Sec-WebSocket-Key');
    }

    $key = base64_encode(sha1($request->header['sec-websocket-key'] . '258EAFA5-
E914-47DA-95CA-C5AB0DC85B11', true));

    $headers = [
        'Upgrade' => 'websocket',
        'Connection' => 'Upgrade',
        'Sec-WebSocket-Accept' => $key,
        'Sec-WebSocket-Version' => '13',
    ];

    if (isset($request->header['sec-websocket-protocol'])) {
        $headers['Sec-WebSocket-Protocol'] = $request->header['sec-websocket-
protocol'];
    }

    return $headers;
}

$server->on("start", function (Server $server) {
    echo 'Swoole WebSocket Server is started at http://127.0.0.1:9501' . PHP_EOL;
});

$server->on('Request', function(Request $request, Response $response) use ($users)
{
    parse_str($request->server['query_string'] ?? '', $params);
```

```

    // verifying token
    if (!isset($params ['token']) || !$userId = getUserByToken($users, $params['token'])) {
        $response->end('Invalid token!');
        return;
    }

    $htmlPage = file_get_contents(__DIR__ . DIRECTORY_SEPARATOR . 'index.html');
    $htmlPage = str_replace('{{user-token}}', $users[$userId]['token2'], $htmlPage);
    $response->end($htmlPage);
});

$server->on('handshake', function(Request $request, Response $response) use ($server, &$users) {
    try {
        $headers = processSecWebSocketKey($request);
    } catch (Exception $e) {
        $response->status(400);
        $response->end($e->getMessage());
        return false;
    }

    parse_str($request->server['query_string'] ?? '', $params);

    if (
        !isset($params ['token'])
        || !$userId = getUserByToken($users, $params['token'], true)
    ) {
        $response->status(401);
        $response->end();
        echo "Invalid token!" . PHP_EOL;
        return false;
    }
    $users[$userId]['token2_used'] = true;

    $name = $users[$userId]['name'];

    $server->user_table->set($request->fd, [
        'id' => $request->fd,
        'name' => $name,
    ]);

    $server->defer(function() use ($request, $server, $name) {
        $server->push($request->fd, json_encode([
            'action' => 'set_user_name',
            'user_name' => $name,
```

```
        ]));
    });

    foreach ($headers as $headerKey => $val) {
        $response->header($headerKey, $val);
    }

    $response->status(101);
    $response->end();
    echo 'Connection open: ' . $request->fd . PHP_EOL;
    return true;
});

$server->on('message', function(Server $server, Frame $frame) {
    $user_name = $server->user_table->get($frame->fd, 'name');

    echo 'Received message (' . $user_name . '): ' . $frame->data . PHP_EOL;

    $addMessage = new AddMessage;
    $deleteMessage = new DeleteMessage;

    Conveyor::init()
        ->server($server)
        ->fd($frame->fd)
        ->persistence()
        ->addActions([$addMessage, $deleteMessage])
        ->addMiddlewareToAction($deleteMessage->getName(), new
DeleteMessageMiddleware)
        ->run($frame->data);
});

$server->on('close', function(Server $server, $fd) {
    echo 'Connection close: ' . $fd . PHP_EOL;
    $server->user_table->del($fd);
});

$server->start();
```

Reference in the repo: https://phpa.me/jacked-php-chapter-5-example5-websocket-server

The handshake

At this server code, we can start by looking at the handshake event, which consists of the most significant difference from the previous example. As said before, we verify the purpose of the connection using the function `processSecWebSocketKey` created previously in the code.

That function will guarantee that this connection has the purpose of a WebSocket connection[12].

In this handshake, we expect a callback token to authorize the user to connect correctly. The token we are expecting there will serve for us to be able to determine the user name, bind this user with the connection, and get the valid single-use token for the WebSocket connection. For that, we grab that information based on the token using our data repository (for simplicity, in this example, the repository happens to be an array) and persist the data about the user in the user_table `OpenSwoole\Table` instance.

For us to share that information with the client, we need to prepare a push to the client with that information (the user name). That happens asynchronously by the usage of the server's method `defer`[13], used in this context because, at the moment of the handshake, the connection is not complete yet, so we have to defer the message to be sent to the client to the end of the event loop:

```
// ...
$server->defer(function() use ($request, $server, $name) {
    $server->push($request->fd, json_encode([
        'action' => 'set_user_name',
        'user_name' => $name,
    ]));
});
// ...
```

Listing 5.12: Deferring the message to the client.

After that, we set the proper headers prepared after the `processSecWebSocketKey` method call and responded with status 101 (meaning the connection was successful).

The token strategy

As you can see in the `$users` global array (that is our repository sample), we will have a primary and secondary token to be used only once by the WebSocket server. The primary token, in the given example, doesn't have usage limits, but the second has. The intent is to secure the connection, requiring some formal HTTP authorization ahead of time.

[12] *https://developer.mozilla.org/en-US/docs/Web/HTTP/Protocol_upgrade_mechanism*
[13] *https://openswoole.com/docs/modules/swoole-server-defer*

The web page

There are some changes to the front end as well, but those are just to adapt to the new situation as the user's name, differently from Case 1, is now set by the authorized user, not by a prompt on the web page.

You can see the latest version of the web page in Listing 5.12:

```
<!DOCTYPE html>
<html>
<head>
    <title>Sample Socket Client UI</title>
</head>
<body>

    <div class="container">

        <h1>WebSocket Client <span id="user_name"></span></h1>

        <form id="message-form">
            <div>
                <textarea id="message-box"></textarea>
            </div>
            <div>
                <input type="submit" />
            </div>
        </form>

        <hr/>

        <ul id="output"></ul>

    </div>

    <script type="text/javascript">

        (function() {

            /**
             * App State.
             */
            var state = {
                user_name: null,
            };

            /**
```

```
                 * App Events.
                 */
                var events = {
                    SET_USER_NAME: 'set_user_name',
                };

                /**
                 * App Core.
                 */
                var app = {
                    ws: null,

                    config: {
                        uri: 'ws://127.0.0.1',
                        port: 9501,
                    },

                    /**
                     *
                     */
                    init: () => {
                        app.listenEvents();
                        app.connectToServer();
                    },

                    /**
                     *
                     */
                    listenEvents: () => {
                        document.getElementById('message-form').addEventListener('submit', app.handleFormSubmit, false);
                        document.addEventListener(events.SET_USER_NAME, app.setUserName, false)
                    },

                    /**
                     *
                     */
                    connectToServer: () => {
                        if (app.ws !== null) {
                            if (!confirm('There is an active connection, do you wish to close it?')) {
                                return;
                            } else {
                                app.ws.close();
                                app.ws = null;
                            }
```

```
           }

           var wsServer = app.config.uri
               + ':'
               + app.config.port
               + '/?token={{user-token}}';
           app.ws = new WebSocket(wsServer);

           app.ws.onopen = function (evt) {
               console.log("Connected to WebSocket server.");
           };

           app.ws.onclose = function (evt) {
               console.log("Disconnected");
               app.ws = null;
               console.log(evt.reason);
           };

            app.ws.onmessage = function (evt) {
                console.log('Received data from server: ' + evt.data);
                app.handleIncomingMessage(evt.data);
            };

            app.ws.onerror = function (evt) {
                console.log('Error occured: ' + evt.data);
            };
        },

        /**
         * @param {Event} e
         */
        handleFormSubmit: (e) => {
            e.preventDefault();
            app.ws.send(JSON.stringify({
                action: 'add-message',
                message: document.getElementById('message-box').value
            }));
        },

        removeMessage: (messageId) => {
            app.ws.send(JSON.stringify({
                action: 'delete-message',
                message_id: messageId
            }));
        },

        /**
```

```
         * @param {String} data
         */
        handleIncomingMessage: (data) => {
            const parsedData = JSON.parse(data);

            switch (parsedData.action) {

                case "add-message":
                    let messageItem = app.createMessageItem(parsedData);
                    messageItem.appendChild(app.createDeleteMessageButton(parsedData));
                    document.getElementById('output').appendChild(messageItem);
                    break;

                case "delete-message":
                    document.getElementById("message-" + parsedData.delete_message_id).remove();
                    break;

                case "error":
                    alert(parsedData['message']);
                    break;

                case "set_user_name":
                    document.dispatchEvent(new CustomEvent(events.SET_USER_NAME, {
                        detail: {
                            user_name: parsedData.user_name
                        }
                    }));
                    break;

                default:
                    console.log("Not recognized message received: " . data);
                    break;
            }
        },

        createMessageItem: (data) => {
            let input = document.createElement("li");
            input.id = "message-" + data.id;
            input.innerHTML = data.message;
            return input;
        },

```

```
                createDeleteMessageButton: (data) => {
                    let button = document.createElement("a");

                    button.title = "Remove message";
                    button.innerHTML = "X";
                    Object.assign(button.style, {
                        marginLeft: "10px",
                        color: "red",
                        fontWeight: "bold",
                        fontFamily: "Sans-Serif"
                    });

                    button.onclick = (e) => {
                        app.removeMessage(data.id);
                    };

                    return button;
                },


                /**
                 * @param {Event} event
                 */
                setUserName: (event) => {
                    document.getElementById('user_name').innerText = '- ' + event.detail.user_name;
                },
            };

            app.init();
        })();

    </script>

</body>
</html>
```

Reference in the repo: https://phpa.me/jacked-php-chapter-5-example5-index

With that in place, the steps to test this example are:

1. Install composer dependencies: `composer install`
2. Start the server: `php websocket-server.php`
3. Open the web page: `http://localhost:9501/?token=123456` (or `http://localhost:9501/?token=7891011` for the other user)

Final Words

PHP developers must familiarize themselves with WebSocket technology, especially for real-time programming. WebSocket's reactive and asynchronous nature presents a departure from traditional PHP programming approaches. PHP developers should explore tools like OpenSwoole to integrate this technology effectively, simplifying the process. Hands-on experience with WebSocket through practice is crucial before it is implemented in client projects.

Chapter

6

Coroutines and Efficient Task Management

Access the chapter examples here: https://phpa.me/jacked-php-chapter-6-examples

Picture yourself waiting in line at a bank, where each teller serves one customer at a time. With two tellers and fourteen customers ahead of you, each taking an average of 10 minutes to be served, you're looking at a 70-minute wait. However, if each teller could handle an additional customer simultaneously, the wait time could be reduced to 35 minutes—a significant improvement.

This scenario mirrors the challenges faced in programming. Running tasks sequentially, where a queue of 10 tasks each takes 1 second, results in a 10-second execution time. For businesses where performance is crucial, finding innovative solutions to enhance efficiency is vital.

There are several solutions available for overcoming these limitations. OpenSwoole is one of the PHP extensions offering such flexibility, alongside Pthreads[1], Parallel[2], and Fibers[3]. At the time of writing, Pthreads had been deprecated, and Parallel had not been updated for a few years. Fibers, on the other hand, is gaining popularity. Alternatives that don't require extension installation include queues, which process tasks asynchronously, allowing for faster completion by assigning multiple workers. The Laravel framework employs this strategy with various drivers, including databases and Redis, though it necessitates additional infrastructure. [4]

The trade-off between using PHP extensions like OpenSwoole for coroutine-based multitasking and implementing a queue-based architecture involves evaluating the complexity of maintaining additional infrastructure against the streamlined simplicity and direct integration of OpenSwoole's solution. They serve differently and must be measured based on workload, performance, maintainability, and performance. While queues provide a robust solution for asynchronous task execution, catering to a broader range of use cases with event-based design, they necessitate dedicated services for message monitoring and storage solutions. This requirement might be overkill for more straightforward tasks, where parallel execution of loop iterations could suffice. OpenSwoole offers an integrated approach, enabling parallel processing without external infrastructure. Its `OpenSwoole\Server` class has a Coroutine Context, allowing immediate Coroutine execution and facilitating a seamless transition to more efficient PHP application development.

Understanding Coroutines

Coroutines are like lightweight threads, but they operate differently. They work in user mode, meaning they use less of the computer's hardware resources than traditional threads that require more direct control from the operating system. This results in coroutines being faster and more efficient to create, destroy, and switch between tasks due to lower overhead.

---

[1] https://www.php.net/manual/en/book.pthreads.php
[2] https://www.php.net/manual/en/book.parallel.php
[3] https://www.php.net/manual/en/language.fibers.php
[4] https://laravel.com/docs/11.x/queues

However, coroutines have a limitation: they don't naturally support multitasking across multiple CPU cores since they run in user space. OpenSwoole addresses this using a multi-process approach, allowing coroutines to utilize multiple cores effectively.

In essence, coroutines are sophisticated functions meant for multitasking without interrupting the flow of tasks based on priority. They enable you to pause and resume parts of a program cooperatively. It is invaluable for performing other tasks while waiting for input/output operations, like data retrieval from a database. This switching capability promotes concurrency, enhancing program efficiency.

OpenSwoole takes advantage of coroutines by assigning one to each server request. It includes a coroutine scheduler that automatically manages when to switch between coroutines based on their input/output status. This switch brings several advantages:

- It allows developers to code as if they were writing synchronous, straightforward PHP code while benefiting from asynchronous input/output efficiencies.
- It reduces the need for complex, nested callbacks, making maintaining code more accessible.
- OpenSwoole's approach is more intuitive than PHP's yield/generator-based coroutines, as it automatically handles most of the input/output switching.
- OpenSwoole provides various coroutine-powered tools (like HTTP Server, HTTP Client, MySQL Client, and Redis Client) that improve performance across different applications.

Consider a situation where our services depend on external data sources. Each external request could take a significant amount of time, affecting the total response time of a request. As illustrated in the following example figures, by multitasking independent procedures, we can reduce the total processing time to that of the longest single step rather than the cumulative time of all steps.

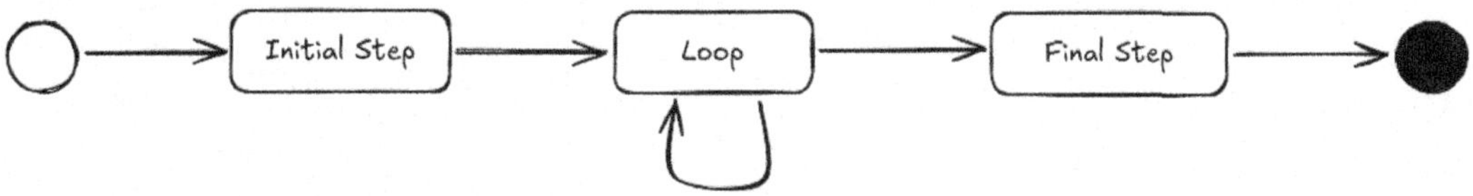

Figure 6.1: Normal synchronous processing of data

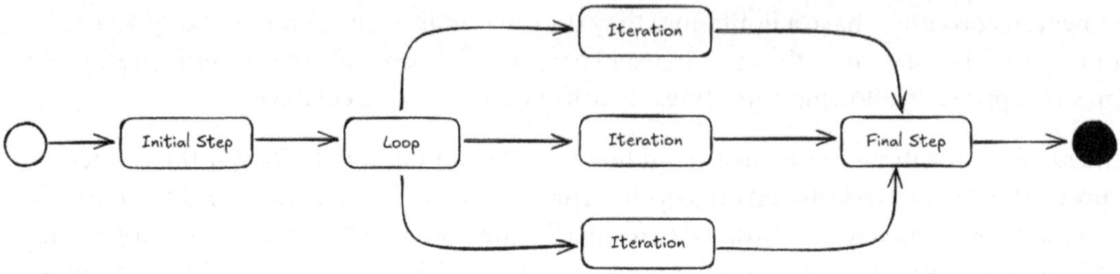

Figure 6.2: Multitasking process of data

To illustrate this concept with numbers, imagine a scenario where our code needs to make 10 external requests in a loop. If each request takes 1 second to complete, then according to the process depicted in Figure 6.1, the total time required would be 10 seconds, plus any additional time needed for other parts of the process. In contrast, the process shown in Figure 6.2 would only take 1 second, assuming all requests are made simultaneously.

> **Important**: *Given the above, it's crucial to benchmark your code to ensure that multitasking is truly enhancing its performance. If your code's iterations involve non-blocking operations or intensive processing, the overhead of switching contexts for multitasking may not justify the effort.*

Example Introduction

Let's dive into this concept with some practical exercises. We will develop two sample applications: the first will act as a server, providing JSON data, and the second will be a client, consuming and processing this JSON data. Through this, we will evaluate memory and time consumption and present some benchmarks to assess performance.

Before we start, there are a couple of important considerations when working with multitasking in OpenSwoole:

1. **HTTP Server Context**: In our case, we are deploying our application on an HTTP server, which inherently provides a certain context that makes the explicit declaration of a "Coroutine Context" (using `co::run()` or `OpenSwoole\Coroutine::run()`) unnecessary. It's unnecessary because the OpenSwoole Server already includes a Coroutine context. If you need clarification on whether an object has this context, the best place to check is the OpenSwoole documentation or OpenSwoole public forums.
2. **Coroutine Support in PHP Libraries**: PHP's core libraries do not natively support coroutines. To integrate them, we use "Coroutine Hooks." These hooks adapt standard PHP functions to work within coroutines. Specifically, for our examples involving CURL for network requests, we will use the following hook: `co::set(['hook_flags' => OpenSwoole\Runtime::HOOK_NATIVE_CURL]);`. For more details on how coroutine hooks work and their compatibility, visit the OpenSwoole documentation at https://openswoole.com/docs/modules/swoole-runtime-flags.

Now, let's proceed with creating a simple server that will send JSON data, as shown in Listing 6.1:

```
<?php

use OpenSwoole\HTTP\Server;
use OpenSwoole\Http\Response;
use OpenSwoole\Http\Request;
use OpenSwoole\Coroutine as Co;

$server = new Server('0.0.0.0', 8080, Server::POOL_MODE);

$server->on('start', function (Server $server) {
    $pid_file = __DIR__ . '/http-server-pid';
    if (file_exists($pid_file)) {
        unlink($pid_file);
    }
    file_put_contents($pid_file, $server->master_pid);
    echo 'Server started with PID: ' . $server->master_pid .
          ' at http://127.0.0.1:' . $server->port . PHP_EOL;
});

$server->on('request', function (Request $request, Response $response) {
    $response->header('Content-Type', 'application/json');

    Co::sleep(1);
    echo 'Executing...' . PHP_EOL;

    if (isset($request->get['user'])) {
        $response->end(json_encode([
            1 => [
                'title' => 'title 1',
                'content' => 'some content',
            ],
            2 => [
                'title' => 'title 2',
                'content' => 'some content 2',
            ],
        ]));
    } else {
        $response->end(json_encode([
            1 => [
                'name' => 'John Galt',
                'email' => 'john@galt.com',
            ],
```

```
            2 => [
                'name' => 'Luke Skywalker',
                'email' => 'luke@skywalker.com',
            ],
            3 => [
                'name' => 'Luke Skywalker 2',
                'email' => 'luke@skywalker2.com',
            ],
        ]));
    }
});

$server->start();
```

Listing 6.1: Sample server for our example (`server.php`).

Reference in the repo: https://phpa.me/jacked-php-chapter-6-example-server-1

> *Notice that we used `Co::sleep` function. This function will block the process for that given time (1 second). If you want to use native functions like `sleep`, `file_get_contents` and PDO related, you'll need to use coroutine hooks. For that, refer to their documentation here: https://openswoole.com/docs/modules/swoole-runtime-flags.*

With that server in mind, let's see in Listing 6.2 the code that executes synchronously a sequence of requests to get, first, the list of users, then a list of posts for each user.

```php
<?php

include __DIR__ . '/vendor/autoload.php';

use OpenSwoole\Core\Coroutine\WaitGroup;
use OpenSwoole\Http\Server;
use OpenSwoole\Http\Response;
use OpenSwoole\Http\Request;
use OpenSwoole\Runtime;

Co::set(['hook_flags' => Runtime::HOOK_NATIVE_CURL]);

$server = new Server('0.0.0.0', 8181, SWOOLE_PROCESS);

$server->on('start', function (Server $server) {
    $pid_file = __DIR__ . '/http-server-pid2';
    if (file_exists($pid_file)) {
        unlink($pid_file);
    }
    file_put_contents($pid_file, $server->master_pid);
    echo 'Server started with PID: ' . $server->master_pid
        . ' at http://127.0.0.1:'    . $server->port . PHP_EOL;
});

function get_users(): array {
    $ch = curl_init();
    curl_setopt($ch, CURLOPT_URL, 'localhost:8080');
    curl_setopt($ch, CURLOPT_RETURNTRANSFER, 1);
    $data = curl_exec($ch);
    curl_close($ch);
    return json_decode($data, true);
}

function get_users_posts(string $email): array {
    $ch = curl_init();
    curl_setopt($ch, CURLOPT_URL, 'localhost:8080?user=1');
    curl_setopt($ch, CURLOPT_RETURNTRANSFER, 1);
    $data = curl_exec($ch);
    curl_close($ch);
    return json_decode($data, true);
}

```

```
$server->on('request', function (Request $request, Response $response) {
    $wg = new WaitGroup();

    $start = microtime(true);

    /** @var array{name: string, email: string} $users */
    $users = get_users(); // ~1 sec

    foreach ($users as $key => $user) {
        go(function () use (&$users, $user, $key, $wg) {
            $wg->add();
            $posts = get_users_posts($user['email']); // ~1 sec
            $users[$key]['posts'] = $posts;
            $wg->done();
        });
    }

    $wg->wait(5);

    $end = microtime(true);

    echo 'Execution Time: ' . ($end - $start) . PHP_EOL;

    $response->end(json_encode($users));
});

$server->start();
```

Listing 6.2: Server that executes some requests to put together users and their posts (`server2.php`).

Reference in the repo: https://phpa.me/jacked-php-chapter-6-example-server-2

When we run the `server2.php` script (accessed via `http://localhost:8181`), the response is typically received within 2 seconds. This delay is due to the `Co::sleep(1)` function in the first server, which postpones each request by 1 second. During a request to `server2.php`, the system fetches user data with one request, taking 1 second. It then retrieves all posts for each user simultaneously, requiring an additional second regardless of the number of users. This parallel processing significantly reduces waiting time; instead of accumulating seconds for each user, all user posts are fetched within just one additional second.

When implementing coroutine functionality, keep these points in mind:

> *Note that closures within `go()` do not automatically share the same variable scope as their surrounding context. To use external variables inside, include them using the `use` keyword and pass them by reference if changes need to reflect outside the closure, like `$users` in our case.*

1. **Enable Coroutine with Native Curl**: If you're using PHP's native `curl` function, activate coroutines using `Swoole\Runtime::enableCoroutine(SWOOLE_HOOK_NATIVE_CURL)`. More information about hooks can be found here: https://openswoole.com/docs/modules/swoole-runtime-flags.
2. **Parallel Execution**: For tasks that should run concurrently, enclose them within the `go()` function. More details on the `go` function are available here: https://openswoole.com/docs/modules/swoole-coroutine#coroutine-example.
3. **Synchronize with WaitGroup**: Use `OpenSwoole\Core\Coroutine\WaitGroup` to complete all asynchronous tasks before sending the final response. When using the `wait` method of `WaitGroup`, you can set a timeout to define the maximum wait time for your response. Learn more about `WaitGroup` at: https://openswoole.com/docs/modules/swoole-coroutine-waitgroup.

To run this example using Docker, use the following command:

```
docker run -d --rm -v $(pwd):/app -p 8080:8080 -p 8181:8181 $(docker build -q .)
```

> **Important**: *OpenSwoole [5] comes with some components that you must enable, and is not always easy to put them together on any Operational System. Due to that, I recommend using a docker environment where you have that sorted out, the swoole image is a good one.*
>
> *Note that if you are requesting from the browser (the recommended), you might get 2 requests reaching your server. You can inspect your browser's requests, and that might show a secondary request to the favicon. If you want to avoid that, you can use a tool like `curl` or `wget` to make the request.*

[5] *https://openswoole.com/docs*

Advanced Multitasking with Coroutines

In the previous section, we explored the basics of coroutines, a form of multitasking used in OpenSwoole. Unlike traditional threading that relies heavily on the operating system, coroutines operate in user space. This approach may not harness the full power of multithreading available at the system level, but it significantly enhances the performance of PHP code by enabling efficient multitasking.

The examples provided demonstrated how coroutines can boost performance, especially when handling multiple tasks simultaneously. However, those were relatively straightforward scenarios. OpenSwoole's coroutines are capable of handling much more complex situations.

Consider a scenario where our tasks involve multiple levels of processing. For instance, in addition to fetching posts as in the previous example, imagine we also need to collect comments for these posts from social media or another API within our infrastructure. In this more complex case, we can initiate additional sub-coroutines specifically for processing these comments within one coroutine that fetches posts.

This setup introduces a new multitasking layer, adding depth to our initial example. Visually, this can be represented as an extension of Figure 6.2, now enhanced with an additional processing layer as depicted in Figure 6.3:

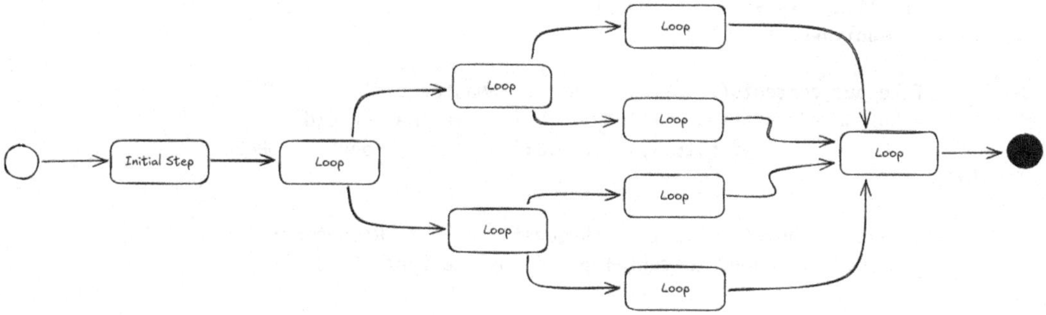

Figure 6.3: Coroutines with sub coroutines

We can integrate additional coroutine contexts into the existing structure to enhance our approach. After retrieving the posts, we will initiate further requests to fetch comments for each post using the same multitasking strategy. Here's how we proceed:

1. We introduce a new wait group for this additional processing layer. This extra layer ensures all coroutines dedicated to fetching comments are complete before moving on.
2. We create a simulated "extra endpoint" within our server to handle comment retrieval. In this context, an "extra endpoint" doesn't refer to a separate physical endpoint but rather a different branch of logic within the same server endpoint.

The updated version of our first server for this advanced scenario is outlined in Listing 6.3:

```php
<?php

use OpenSwoole\HTTP\Server;
use OpenSwoole\Http\Response;
use OpenSwoole\Http\Request;
use OpenSwoole\Coroutine as Co;

$server = new Server('0.0.0.0', 8080, Server::POOL_MODE);

$server->on('start', function (Server $server) {
    $pid_file = __DIR__ . '/http-server-pid';
    if (file_exists($pid_file)) {
        unlink($pid_file);
    }
    file_put_contents($pid_file, $server->master_pid);
    echo 'Server started with PID: ' . $server->master_pid
            . ' at http://127.0.0.1:' . $server->port . PHP_EOL;
});

$server->on('request', function (Request $request, Response $response) {
    $response->header('Content-Type', 'application/json');

    Co::sleep(1);
    echo 'Executing...' . PHP_EOL;

    if (isset($request->get['user'])) {
        $response->end(json_encode([
            1 => [
                'title' => 'title 1',
                'content' => 'some content',
            ],
            2 => [
                'title' => 'title 2',
                'content' => 'some content 2',
```

```
                ],
            ]));
        } else {
            $response->end(json_encode([
                1 => [
                    'name' => 'John Galt',
                    'email' => 'john@galt.com',
                ],
                2 => [
                    'name' => 'Luke Skywalker',
                    'email' => 'luke@skywalker.com',
                ],
                3 => [
                    'name' => 'Luke Skywalker 2',
                    'email' => 'luke@skywalker2.com',
                ],
            ]));
        }
});

$server->start();
```

Listing 6.3: Post's comments implementation at the second version of the server 1.

Reference in the repo: https://phpa.me/jacked-php-chapter-6-exampler-server-v2

The second version of the server 2 is as shown in Listing 6.4:

```
<?php

include __DIR__ . '/vendor/autoload.php';

use OpenSwoole\Core\Coroutine\WaitGroup;
use OpenSwoole\Http\Server;
use OpenSwoole\Http\Response;
use OpenSwoole\Http\Request;
use OpenSwoole\Runtime;
use OpenSwoole\Coroutine as Co;

Co::set(['hook_flags' => Runtime::HOOK_NATIVE_CURL]);

$server = new Server('0.0.0.0', 8181, Server::POOL_MODE);

$server->set([
    'enable_coroutine' => true,
    'max_coroutine' => 3000,
```

```
]);

$server->on('start', function (Server $server) {
    $pid_file = __DIR__ . '/http-server-pid2';
    if (file_exists($pid_file)) {
        unlink($pid_file);
    }
    file_put_contents($pid_file, $server->master_pid);
    echo 'Server started with PID: ' . $server->master_pid . ' at http://127.0.0.1:'
. $server->port . PHP_EOL;
});

function curl_request(string $url): array
{
    $ch = curl_init();
    curl_setopt($ch, CURLOPT_URL, $url);
    curl_setopt($ch, CURLOPT_RETURNTRANSFER, 1);
    $data = curl_exec($ch);
    curl_close($ch);
    return json_decode($data, true);
}

function get_users(): array
{
    return curl_request("localhost:8080");
}

function get_users_posts(string $email): array
{
    return curl_request("localhost:8080?user=1");
}

function get_posts_comments(int $post_id): array
{
    return curl_request("localhost:8080?post_id=" . $post_id);
}

$server->on('request', function (Request $request, Response $response) {
    $wg = new WaitGroup();

    $start = microtime(true);

    $users = get_users(); // ~1 sec

    foreach ($users as $key => $user) {
        go(function () use (&$users, $user, $key, $wg, $start) {
            $wg->add();
```

```
                $posts = get_users_posts($user['email']); // ~1 sec

                $wg2 = new WaitGroup();

                foreach ($posts as $post_id => $post) {
                    go(function () use (&$posts, $post_id, $wg2) {
                        $wg2->add();
                        $comments = get_posts_comments($post_id); // ~1 sec
                        $posts[$post_id]['comments'] = $comments;
                        $wg2->done();
                    });
                }

                $wg2->wait(5);

                $users[$key]['posts'] = $posts;
                $wg->done();
            });
        }

        $wg->wait(5);

        $end = microtime(true);

        echo 'Execution Time: ' . ($end - $start) . PHP_EOL;

        $response->end(json_encode($users));
    });

    $server->start();
```

Listing 6.4: Post's comments being retrieved at the second version of the server 2.

Reference in the repo: https://phpa.me/jacked-php-chapter-6-example2-server-v2

> *Notice that we added a small code improvement to avoid repeating too much code: we reused the curl procedure call and shrinked the functions that knows the url for each call to a minimum.*

At these second versions of each server example we added only 1 second by adding further requests that cost 1 second each. The total will be 3 seconds.

Communication between Coroutines

Via OpenSwoole Channel

We saw in the previous examples strategies to implement coroutines so we can proceed with expensive parallel requests without them affecting the performance of the code too much. That covers one case, but there are other cases. We have a case where one coroutine must communicate with the other. One of the options for that is to use OpenSwoole Channel.

As in the previous chapters and sections, the examples for this section are at the repository, example 2 of chapter 6: https://github.com/Jacked-PHP/jacked-php-book-examples/tree/0379a2516054ee6d0282fb88527102cda3f1acd5/06-examples/example2

Now imagine we are getting data from one coroutine and have another printing this data to a command line. In such cases, when we push data into a channel, any coroutine waiting for it gets notified and can do something with it. It would be similar to what is shown at the Figure 6.4:

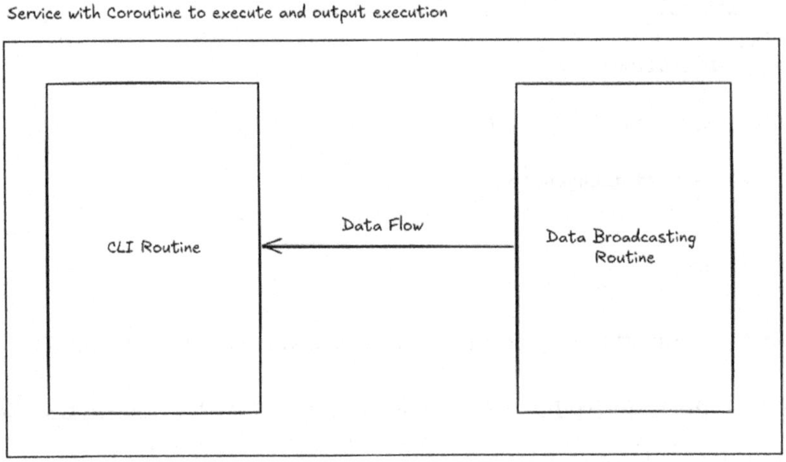

Figure 6.4: Service broadcasting to the command line interface

In this example, we only need one `service.php` file and a file from which we will read the data (or we could quickly adapt a request to the server serving the data in the previous section). In this example, the coroutine broadcasting the data will be reading the data from a local file. The coroutine displaying the data will be reading the data from a channel used by both coroutines. The goal is mainly to sync data between coroutines according to requirements so the data produced or gathered in one coroutine is available in another.

In Listing 6.5 you can see the implementation of this case:

```php
<?php

use OpenSwoole\Coroutine as Co;
use OpenSwoole\Coroutine\Channel;

$chan = new Channel(1);

function get_users(): array
{
    $raw_data = file_get_contents(__DIR__ . '/data.json');
    return json_decode($raw_data, true);
}

Co::run(function () use ($chan) {

    // Coroutine producing data.
    go(function () use ($chan) {
        $i = 0;
        while (1) {
            system('clear');
            echo $i . PHP_EOL;
            Co::sleep(1.0);
            $users = get_users();
            foreach ($users as $user) {
                $chan->push($user['name']);
                Co::sleep(1.0);
            }
            Co::sleep(10.0);
            $i++;
        }
    });

    // Coroutine printing data.
    go(function () use ($chan) {
        while (1) {
            $user_name = $chan->pop();
            echo 'User:' . $user_name . PHP_EOL;
        }
    });

});
```

Listing 6.5: service.php that gather data from file and present it using different coroutines.

Reference in the repo: https://phpa.me/jacked-php-chapter-6-example2-service

Use cases for this go from monitoring services to syncing data between different services with a specific frequency.

This communication can be from any nature of service that serves data. We can enhance how it presents that data in this example in different ways, such as pulling data from other sources like websites crawling or APIs, publishing that on social media, or dispatching alerts via email or text messages if/when needed.

At Listing 6.5, the service streams users retrieved from a file. For each user sent to the other coroutine, the data sent gets presented. After displaying each user name, the first coroutine waits 10 seconds and clears the command line. After that, it does the same until the process is killed on an infinite loop. The execution has a counter displayed in each iteration's first line. The Figure 6.5 will show one of the iterations of the output:

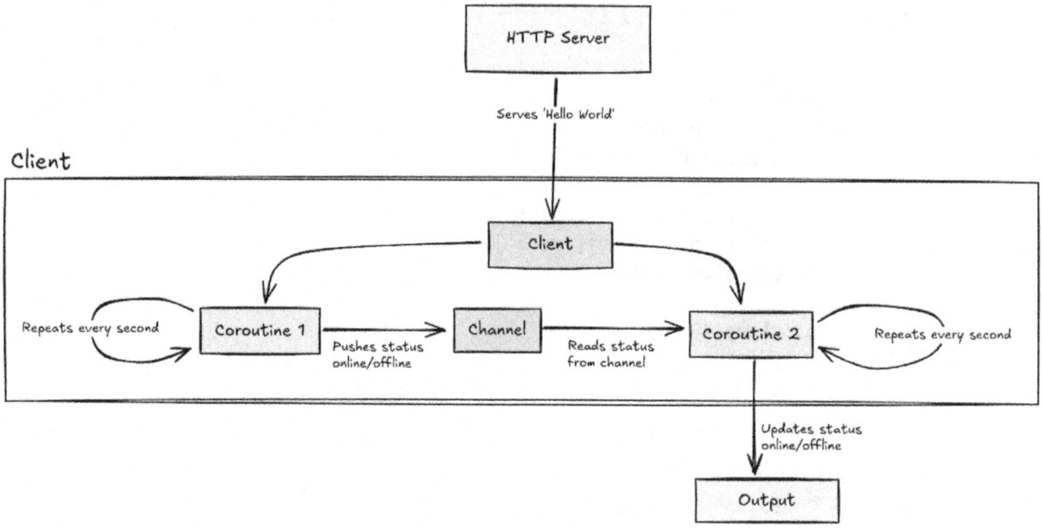

Figure 6.5: Iteration 4 of the inifinite loop streaming user names.

A more complex example based on Listing 6.5 would be what is shown in Listing 6.6:

```php
<?php

use OpenSwoole\Coroutine as Co;
use OpenSwoole\Coroutine\Channel;

// Let's ignore warnings to keep the screen clean.
error_reporting(E_ERROR | E_PARSE);

function check_site(): bool
{
    ini_set('default_socket_timeout', '05');
    set_time_limit(5);
    $f = fopen('http://localhost:8080', 'r');

    if ($f) {
        $r = fread($f, 1000);
        fclose($f);
    }

    if (strlen($r) > 1) {
        return true;
    }

    return false;
}

Co::run(function () {
    $chan = new Channel(1);

    // Coroutine producing data.
    go(function () use ($chan) {
        while (1) {
            $chan->push(['is_online' => check_site()]);
            co::sleep(1.0);
        }
    });

    // Coroutine printing data.
    go(function () use ($chan) {
        $status = null;
        echo 'Starting...' . PHP_EOL;
        while (1) {
            $data = $chan->pop();
            $new_status = $data['is_online'];

```

```
                if ($status !== $new_status) {
                    system('clear');
                    echo 'Status: ' . ($new_status ? 'Online' : 'Offline') . PHP_EOL;
                    // here we can send a message via bot, text, email...
                    $status = $new_status;
                }

                Co::sleep(1.0);
            }
        });

});
```

Listing 6.6: service2.php that checks if a website is online and present using different coroutines.

Reference in the repo: https://phpa.me/jacked-php-chapter-6-example2-service2

```
<?php

use OpenSwoole\Http\Server;
use OpenSwoole\Http\Request;
use OpenSwoole\Http\Response;

$server = new Server('0.0.0.0', 8080);

$server->on('start', function (Server $server) {
    echo 'Swoole http server is started at http://0.0.0.0:8080' . PHP_EOL;
});

$server->on('request', function (Request $request, Response $response) {
    $response->header('Content-Type', 'text/plain');
    $response->end('Hello World' . PHP_EOL);
});

$server->start();
```

Listing 6.7: test_server.php with the test server for the service 2 shown in the Listing 6.6.

Reference in the repo: https://phpa.me/jacked-php-chapter-6-example2-test-server

To run it, start the server test with `php test_server.php` (shown in Listing 6.7), and in a parallel terminal, execute service 2: `service2.php`. If you turn off the `test_server.php`, you'll see "Offline"; if you turn it on, you'll see "Online".

At this service, you can see that the overall structure remains the same with different procedures.

Via yield/resume

This approach for the communication between coroutines is different and is helpful for when you have points in the execution that you need another coroutine to take over. You can invoke another coroutine using the method `OpenSwoole\Coroutine::yield`.

One example of this implementation would be to have a specific order of events. Having one coroutine responsible for preparing the data while the other makes further external requests can give a pretty good idea of how it works and how to use it. Figure 6.6 shows a usage where we delegate to one coroutine the retrieval of the data and to the other coroutine the preparation for the next step.

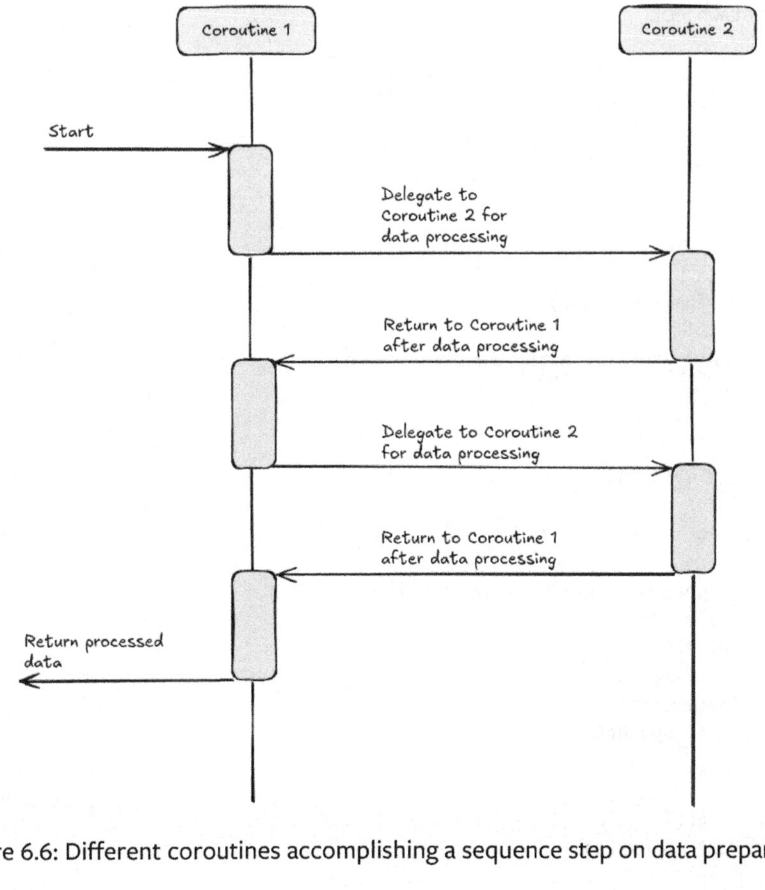

Figure 6.6: Different coroutines accomplishing a sequence step on data preparation.

To accomplish this, we have a code that yields to the other available coroutine so the process can continue there.

> **Important**: *if you yield and don't resume at some point, you cause deadlock. Always keep that in mind.*

The code at Listing 6.8 has the implementation for a case like the diagram above:

```
#!/usr/bin/env php
<?php
declare(strict_types=1);

use OpenSwoole\Coroutine as Co;

class DataObject
{
    public $total = 0;
    public $data = [];

    public function push($item)
    {
        $this->data[] = $item;
    }

    public function sum()
    {
        $this->total = array_sum($this->data);
    }
}

$data = new DataObject;

Co::run(function () use (&$data) {

    $co1 = go(function () use (&$data) {
        $data->push(1);
        Co::yield();
        $data->push(3);
        Co::yield();
        $data->push(5);
    });

    $co2 = go(function () use (&$data) {
        $data->push(2);
```

```
        Co::yield();
        $data->push(4);
        Co::yield();
        $data->push(6);
    });

    // process
    Co::resume($co1);
    Co::resume($co2);
    Co::resume($co1);
    Co::resume($co2);

});

echo implode(',', $data->data) . PHP_EOL;
```

Listing 6.8: Implementation of yield/resume strategy.

Reference in the repo: https://phpa.me/jacked-php-chapter-6-example3-service

In Listing 6.8, the context starts around the coroutines that will be waiting for the other coroutines to take action. That happens with the `OpenSwoole\Coroutine::yield()` call that gives the "turn" to the next `OpenSwoole\Coroutine::resume()` call, causing the insertion of the numbers to happen in sequence.

The output will be `1,2,3,4,5,6`.

Final Words

Coroutines are a big game changer to PHP performance. By properly executing coroutines, the application may become faster. One of the tradeoffs is the complexity, so use it wisely: only some cases are suitable for multitasking. An essential aspect is if a given case is worthy of coroutines - sometimes, coroutines increase the time consumed by a task. The extra time comes from coroutines. They consume some time for context change. That said, it is always a good thing to measure the tradeoffs before making a final decision.

Chapter 7

Process Management

Examples of this chapter:
https://phpa.me/jacked-php-chapter-7-examples

Imagine you are responsible for maintaining a web application that must handle high traffic efficiently in a development environment. The web server must be started, monitored, and stopped based on varying traffic loads and maintenance schedules. Ensuring the server is up and running or properly shut down when necessary is crucial for maintaining a smooth user experience and optimal server performance.

To achieve this, you need a robust solution that allows you to control the web server processes programmatically. This can be implemented using OpenSwoole's process management capabilities, allowing for granular server operations control. Let's build a sample that combines all the necessary components for such a scenario.

Introduction to Processes

A process is an instance of a program in execution. It is a fundamental concept in operating systems, and Linux is no exception. Each process has its memory space, system resources, and execution context. Processes are managed by the operating system's kernel, which schedules them for execution, allocates resources, and enforces security policies. OpenSwoole integrates with Linux processes to handle concurrent tasks efficiently.

It is possible to control Linux processes using PHP. A common way of doing this is to use the PHP extension PCNTL. This implements the Unix-style process creation, execution, and signal handling. To use it, you need to recompile PHP with it enabled. OpenSwoole has an alternative to that called OpenSwoole Process. The most significant advantage is that it is inside OpenSwoole's ecosystem. The main documentation can be found here: https://openswoole.com/docs/modules/swoole-process.

Now, let's explore its usage in detail. OpenSwoole Process represents a specific Linux Process running on the server. When you start a process using this component, two Linux processes will run on your server: the parent process, which is the PHP file context you are executing, and the child process, which is created using OpenSwoole Process. The base structure is as follows:

```
<?php
use OpenSwoole\Process;

$process = new Process(function(){
    // Here goes what you intend to do with this process.
});

// @var int
$pid = $process->start();
```

Listing 7.1: Basic structure for OpenSwoole Process.

Throughout this chapter, you'll see many aspects of the `OpenSwoole\Process` class, having the opportunity to see details that will allow you to properly control and coordinate multiple Linux Processes to achieve a huge number of possible implementations.

Multiple Processes coordination

Let's explore one example where we have synchronization between multiple processes sharing a Connection Pool:

```php
<?php

include __DIR__ . '/vendor/autoload.php';

use JackedPhp\LiteConnect\Migration\MigrationManager;
use JackedPhp\LiteConnect\SQLiteFactory;
use OpenSwoole\Atomic;
use OpenSwoole\Core\Coroutine\Pool\ClientPool;
use OpenSwoole\Coroutine as Co;
use JackedPhp\LiteConnect\Connection\Connection;
use Migrations\CreateUsersTable;
use Models\User;
use OpenSwoole\Process;

$databasePath = __DIR__ . '/database/database.sqlite';
$connectionPool = new ClientPool(
    factory: SQLiteFactory::class,
    config: [
        'database' => $databasePath,
    ],
    size: 1,
);

function getConnection(ClientPool &$connectionPool): Connection {
    $connection = null;
    Co::run(function() use (&$connection, &$connectionPool) {
        $connection = $connectionPool->get();
    });

    return $connection;
}

function putConnection(ClientPool &$connectionPool, Connection $connection): void {
    Co::run(function() use (&$connection, &$connectionPool) {
        $connectionPool->put($connection);
    });
}

```

```
function runMigrations(Connection $connection): void {
    $migrationManager = new MigrationManager($connection);
    $migrationManager->runMigrations([new CreateUsersTable()]);
}

function createBaseUsers(Connection $connection): void {
    $user = new User($connection);
    $raw_data = file_get_contents(__DIR__ . '/data.json');
    $data = json_decode($raw_data, true);
    foreach ($data as $user_data) {
        $user->create($user_data);
    }
}

// always start fresh
if (file_exists($databasePath)) {
    unlink($databasePath);
    touch($databasePath);
}

$connection = getConnection($connectionPool);
runMigrations($connection);
createBaseUsers($connection);
putConnection($connectionPool, $connection);

// process being here

$counter = new Atomic(0);
$assertionsCounter = new Atomic(0);
$workerNum = 10;
$processes = [];

for ($i = 0; $i < $workerNum; $i++) {
    $process = new Process(function (Process $process) use (
        $workerNum,
        &$connectionPool,
        &$counter,
        &$assertionsCounter
    ) {
        $connection = $connectionPool->get();

        if ($connection->isConnected()) {
            $user = new User($connection);
            $expectedNewName = $process->pid . '-' . $counter->get();

            $currentUser = current($user->get());
            $currentUser->update(['name' => $expectedNewName]);
```

```

            $currentUser = current($user->get());
            if ($expectedNewName !== $currentUser->name) {
                $assertionsCounter->add(1);
            }
        }

        $counter->add(1);
        $connectionPool->put($connection);
        $process->write('bye! (from ' . $process->pid . ')');
    }, enableCoroutine: true);

    $process->useQueue();
    $process->start();
    $processes[$process->pid] = $process;
}

foreach ($processes as $pid => $process) {
    $result = $process->read();
    echo $result . PHP_EOL;
    Process::kill($process->pid);
}

echo '====================' . PHP_EOL;
echo 'Total: ' . $counter->get() . PHP_EOL;
echo 'Assertion Errors: ' . $assertionsCounter->get() . PHP_EOL;
```

Listing 7.2: 10 Processes sharing a Connection Pool of size 1.

Reference: https://phpa.me/jacked-php-chapter-7-example1

Now, let's look at the key components for handling database connections and concurrent processes when working with OpenSwoole and SQLite. The code presented uses OpenSwoole's `ClientPool` to manage database connections. It uses the process feature "Process::useQueue", allowing a queue for reading and writing input/output between the main and sub-processes. It also maintains integrity across multiple workers.

A `ClientPool` is utilized to manage connections to an SQLite database. The `ClientPool` class comes from the OpenSwoole Core package (https://github.com/openswoole/core) and helps manage database connections in a concurrent environment. It allows for a pool of reusable connections, making it especially suitable for scenarios where multiple processes or coroutines need to access the same database.

This is the creation of the connection pool:

```
$connectionPool = new ClientPool(
    factory: SQLiteFactory::class,
    config: [
        'database' => $databasePath,
    ],
    size: 1,
);
```

The `ClientPool` is initialized with a factory class (`SQLiteFactory` - that is part of the package used for this SQLite connection) and a configuration array. The configuration specifies the database path. This pool is given a size of 1, meaning that only one connection to the SQLite database will be managed within the pool. This conservative sizing is due to SQLite's nature as a single-user database for writing. It is not expected to function well for concurrent writes from multiple connections. It is a good idea to keep a small pool to ensure safety in a concurrent environment.

The connection to SQLite is established using a custom library, `LiteConnect` (https://github.com/Jacked-PHP/lite-connect), which allows us to manage connections without relying on global variables. This design choice is important when working with OpenSwoole because globals can introduce issues in a concurrent environment.

Global variables are problematic in coroutine and multiprocessing contexts due to potential conflicts and data integrity issues. In a coroutine-based system, multiple coroutines can run concurrently within the same process. If globals are used, they may be accessed and modified simultaneously by different coroutines, leading to race conditions and unpredictable behaviors. Similarly, in a multi-process environment, each process maintains its own memory space, so sharing global variables between processes becomes non-trivial, often requiring inter-process communication mechanisms that complicate the design.

By using `LiteConnect` and encapsulating the connection in instances, each process or coroutine gets a clean state with its connection object. This makes the code more predictable and easier to manage.

Now let's look at the part of the Listing 7.2 that shows the approach of creating multiple processes using a loop:

```
$workerNum = 10;
$processes = [];

for ($i = 0; $i < $workerNum; $i++) {
    $process = new Process(function (Process $process) use (
        $workerNum,
        &$connectionPool,
        &$counter,
        &$assertionsCounter
    ) {
        // Process logic here...
    }, enableCoroutine: true);

    $process->useQueue();
    $process->start();
    $processes[$process->pid] = $process;
}
```

All these processes will work in parallel. Each process retrieves a database connection from the pool, fetches a user record, and then updates it. After that, it returns the connection to the pool. This approach maximizes the utilization of the single SQLite connection while remaining safe for concurrent operations.

Using multiple processes with a shared connection pool is ideal when working with read-heavy workloads or scenarios where operations must avoid write conflicts. Each process performs a task independently, allowing for parallel processing without risking database integrity.

The `Process::useQueue()` method enables the use of a message queue for communication between the parent process and the child processes. In OpenSwoole, this allows the parent process to send and receive messages from its child processes in a controlled manner:

By using a queue, the process can share messages, such as status updates or operation results, between the worker and the main process. This can coordinate tasks, check for completion, and handle any errors that may arise during execution.

Once `Process::useQueue()` is enabled, processes can write messages to the queue, and the parent process can read those messages. Each child process writes a message to the queue once it finishes its task, which includes updating a user's name in the database. That message can have many objectives. In our case, we want to confirm that the process is done. The parent process then reads this message and proceeds to the next steps.

This communication allows the main process to monitor the completion of each child process and, for example, can ensure that resources, such as the connection from the pool, are properly released—but we are not doing that here for simplicity.

At the end of the script, we see an output summarizing the total number of operations and any assertion errors:

```
echo '====================' . PHP_EOL;
echo 'Total:'. $counter->get() . PHP_EOL;
echo 'Assertion Errors:'. $assertionsCounter->get() . PHP_EOL;
```

One thing to notice is that these counters use `OpenSwoole\Atomic`. They can hold integers for high-performance counter service. That component is excellent for multi-threading synchronization. The `counter` tracks the total number of operations executed by all processes. Each time a worker completes a task, it increments this counter. Meanwhile, `assertion-sCounter` keeps track of any errors in expected behavior, such as a mismatch between an expected and actual value during the name update process. This setup provides a simple yet effective way to monitor the performance and correctness of the multi-process workload.

In the end, this script outputs the total number of updates performed and any errors during the process. This output allows us to verify that the operations were executed correctly and that the concurrent setup worked as intended.

Managing Processes

In our example, we will build a managed WebServer. This process will keep track of the managed server by the process name. The WebServer we will manage is as shown in Listing 7.2:

```php
#!/usr/bin/php

<?php

use OpenSwoole\HTTP\Server;
use OpenSwoole\Http\Request;
use OpenSwoole\Http\Response;
use OpenSwoole\Coroutine\System;
use OpenSwoole\Coroutine as Co;
use OpenSwoole\Util;

include_once __DIR__ . '/constants.php';

Util::setProcessName(HTTP_PROCESS_NAME);

$port = 8181;

$server = new Server('0.0.0.0', $port);
$server->set([
    'worker_num' => 1,
]);
$server->on('start', function (Server $server) use ($port) {
    echo 'OpenSwoole http server is started at http://127.0.0.1:' . $port . PHP_EOL;
});
$server->on('shutdown', function (Server $server) {
    echo 'OpenSwoole http server is shutting down.' . PHP_EOL;
});
$server->on('request', function (Request $request, Response $response) {
    $response->header('Content-Type', 'text/plain');
    $response->end('Hello World' . PHP_EOL);
});
$server->start();

// Listening for the kill signal.
Co::run(function () {
    System::waitSignal(SIGKILL, -1);
});
```

Listing 7.2: HTTP Server example.

The Listing 7.2 is a simple script that starts an HTTP server that listens on port 8181 and responds with "Hello World" to any incoming HTTP request. This will be the server we will control in our example. The server is started by executing the command `php server.php` in the terminal. The server will be running in the background, and we will control it through the parent process.

Then, we will control it via Processes, being able to start and stop it as we want from a web page. A small admin area with real-time data will be available for us to do that. For this requirement, we will use three files and will need five processes in the main service file:

1. **The Main Process** - The file we are executing.
2. **The WebSocket Server Process** - The server for the admin area. This is represented by two items in Figure 7.1: the WebSocket Server and the Admin Interface, which is served by the WebSocket Server and can be visualized in the browser.
3. **The HTTP Server Process** - The server we are managing.
4. **The Monitor Process** - The process that monitors the HTTP Server. It maintains communication between the HTTP Server and the WebSocket Server, ensuring that the admin interface receives real-time updates about the HTTP Server's status and allows us to control it.

In our example, we will use almost all the tools discussed in this book. Feel free to go back when needed to understand specific topics. Figure 7.1 represents the organization and communication between the different processes:

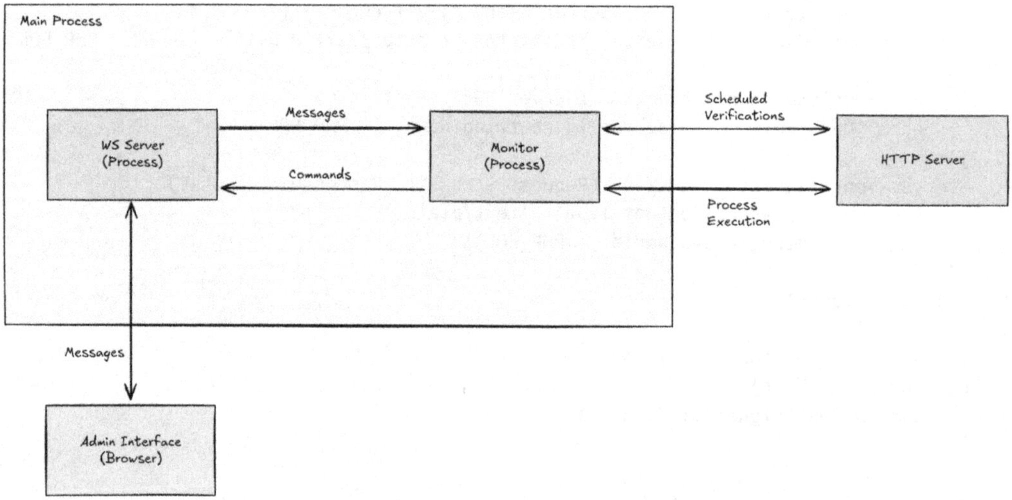

Figure 7.1: Processes Organization and Communication

Shared Memory Communication Strategy

You'll have access to the entire file at the repository. Let's focus on the main parts of the solution. Before jumping into them, let's see the global context.

In multi-process or multi-threaded environments, sharing data between different processes or threads efficiently and safely is crucial. One common strategy to achieve this is through shared memory.

In this solution, we have constants and some global scoped variables in the global context. They will serve the purpose of sharing data between different parts of the app (mainly for reuse). Global variables in PHP are accessible throughout the entire script but are confined to a single process, meaning they cannot be shared directly between different processes or threads.

Our solution aims to coordinate actions cross processes, sharing information and state cross contexts. In this case, we will be using `OpenSwoole\Table` as our Shared Memory solution. These tables are handy for storing and sharing data across different contexts without the need for more complex inter-process communication mechanisms like sockets or message queues.

Key Features:

- High Performance: Accessing and modifying data in an `OpenSwoole\Table` is fast, making it suitable for real-time applications.
- Concurrency: Table is designed to handle concurrent access by multiple processes, ensuring data integrity without requiring explicit locks.

`OpenSwoole\Table` is a specialized data structure that resides in shared memory, allowing multiple processes to access and modify its data concurrently. This makes Table suitable for inter-process communication and data sharing, unlike global variables which are limited to the scope of a single process.

Listing 7.3 shows the `OpenSwoole\Table` that we will be using for this solution:

```php
<?php

namespace ServerManager;

use OpenSwoole\Table;

class Helper
{
    public static function startTable(): Table
    {
        $actions_table = new Table(1024);
        $actions_table->column('data', Table::TYPE_STRING, 64);
        $actions_table->create();

        return $actions_table;
    }

    // ...
}
```

Listing 7.3: Our `OpenSwoole\Table` strategy.

Reference in the repo: https://phpa.me/jacked-php-chapter-7-helper.

The code in Listing 7.3 demonstrates the `Helper` class, which includes a static method startTable that initializes and returns an instance of `OpenSwoole\Table`. This table stores and shares data among various processes in our solution. It features a single column named data, capable of holding up to 64 characters in length string values. The table is configured to accommodate up to 1024 rows, representing the maximum number of rows it can hold.

This `Helper` class encompasses numerous other useful methods employed throughout our solution. The startTable method is merely one example. The `Helper` class serves as a utility class containing methods for common tasks. For more detailed information and additional code samples, refer to the repository mentioned in this chapter.

Multi-Process Strategy

Before proceeding, to facilitate our implementation of processes, we will use an abstraction that allows for the easy creation and management of processes. All our processes will extend this abstraction. The abstraction is shown in Listing 7.4:

```php
<?php

namespace ServerManager;

use OpenSwoole\Process;
use OpenSwoole\Table;
use OpenSwoole\Util;

abstract class ServiceProcess
{
    /** @var array<int> */
    protected array $pids;

    public function __construct(
        protected Table $actionsTable,
    ) {}

    protected function setProcessName(string $name): void
    {
        Util::setProcessName($name);
    }

    public function run(?callable $callback = null): void
    {
        echo "Starting " . static::class . "..." . PHP_EOL;
        $process = new Process(function (Process $worker) use ($callback) {
            if ($callback) {
                $callback();
                return;
            }
            $this->callback();
        });
        $this->pids[] = $process->start();
    }

    abstract public function callback(): void;

    public function stop(): void
    {
        foreach ($this->pids as $pid) {
            Process::kill($pid, SIGKILL);
        }
    }
}
```

Listing 7.4: ServiceProcess abstraction.

Reference in the repo: https://phpa.me/jacked-php-chapter-7-ServiceProcess

The code in Listing 7.4 illustrates the ServiceProcess class, which serves as an abstraction to simplify the creation and management of processes. This class includes several methods:

1. `setProcessName`: This protected method sets the name of the process using OpenSwoole::setProcessName. Setting process names is beneficial for debugging and monitoring, as it allows you to easily identify and distinguish between different processes running on the system.
2. `run`: This public method starts a new process. It accepts an optional callback function, which, if provided, will be executed within the process. If no callback is provided, the abstract callback method, which must be implemented by subclasses, will be executed. This method:

- Prints a message indicating the start of the process.
- Creates a new OpenSwooleinstance, passing a function that either executes the provided callback or the callback method.
- Starts the process and stores the process ID (PID) in the pids array for later management.

3. `callback`: This abstract method must be implemented by any subclass extending ServiceProcess. It is intended to contain the specific logic that the process will execute. By making this method abstract, we enforce that every subclass provides its own implementation of the process logic, ensuring that each process performs its intended function.
4. `stop`: This public method stops all running processes by sending a SIGKILL signal to each process ID stored in the pids array. This method iterates through the pids array and terminates each process, ensuring a clean shutdown of all processes managed by the class.

The ServiceProcess class is designed to be extended by other classes representing specific processes in our solution. By leveraging this abstraction, we can ensure a consistent approach to process management, making it easier to create, run, and stop processes as needed. This abstraction provides a robust framework for process management, promoting code reuse and simplifying the implementation of process-related functionality.

For example, suppose we need to create a process that handles logging. We could make a new LoggingProcess class that extends ServiceProcess and implements the callback method to define the logging logic. Similarly, other processes such as data processing, monitoring, or communication can be implemented by extending ServiceProcess, ensuring that all processes adhere to a consistent interface and behavior.

Using this abstraction, we can manage processes more effectively, reducing redundancy and improving the maintainability of our codebase. The abstraction also allows for flexibility, as the implementation details of each process can be encapsulated within their respective classes, making it easier to modify or extend functionality as needed.

WebSocket Server Process

Now we need some realtime way to make some communication flow between the website and the processes. The communication using Table is a way to keep the communication between the different processes. Between the Admin area and the other processes, we will use a WebSocket Server. That way, we can send commands from the browser, and from the server to the browser, in realtime, making sure that we know asap the current state of the HTTP Server. The WebSocket Server will be inside a Process.

The WebSocket Server inside a Process is shown at the Listing 7.5:

```
<?php

namespace ServerManager;

use League\Plates\Engine;
use OpenSwoole\Coroutine as Co;
use OpenSwoole\Http\Request;
use OpenSwoole\Http\Response;
use OpenSwoole\Table;
use OpenSwoole\Timer;
use OpenSwoole\WebSocket\Frame;
use OpenSwoole\WebSocket\Server;

class WsServer extends ServiceProcess
{
    public function __construct(
        Table $actionsTable,
        protected string $host = '0.0.0.0',
        protected int $port = 8080,
    ) {
        parent::__construct($actionsTable);

        $this->run([$this, 'startReactionTimer']);
    }

    public function callback(): void
    {
        $this->setProcessName(WS_PROCESS_NAME);

```

```
        $server = new Server($this->host, $this->port);

        $server->set([
            'document_root' => ROOT_DIR,
            'enable_static_handler' => true,
            'static_handler_locations' => ['/public'],
        ]);

        $server->on('open', fn (Server $s, Request $r) => $this->onOpen($s, $r));

        $server->on('request', fn (Request $req, Response $res) => $this->onRequest($req, $res));

        $server->on('message', fn (Server $s, Frame $f) => $this->onMessage($s, $f));

        $server->on('close', fn (Server $server, $fd) => $this->onClose($server, $fd));

        $server->start();
    }

    protected function onMessageTick(Server $server, Request $request): void
    {
        $status = $this->actionsTable->get(HTTP_STATUS_TABLE_KEY, 'data');
        $currentState = $this->actionsTable->get(HTTP_TEMP_STATUS_TABLE_KEY, 'data');

        if ($currentState === $status) {
            return;
        }

        echo 'Sending status: ' . $status . PHP_EOL;
        $this->actionsTable->set(HTTP_TEMP_STATUS_TABLE_KEY, [
            'data' => $status,
        ]);

        foreach ($server->connections as $fd) {
            echo "Sending status to: $fd\n";
            if ($server->isEstablished($fd)) {
                $server->push($fd, json_encode([
                    'id' => $fd,
                    'data' => [
                        'event' => 'server-status',
                        'data' => $status,
                    ],
                ]));
```

```
            }
        }
    }

    protected function onReactionTick(): void
    {
        $data = $this->actionsTable->get(WS_TABLE_KEY, 'data');
        $this->actionsTable->del(WS_TABLE_KEY);

        if (!$data) {
            return;
        }

        $parsedData = json_decode($data, true);
        if (!$parsedData) {
            return;
        }

        switch ($parsedData['event']) {
            case 'start':
                Helper::startHttpServer();
                break;
            case 'stop':
                Helper::stopHttpServer();
                break;
            case 'keep-alive':
                Helper::setConfig($this->actionsTable, KEEP_ALIVE, $parsedData['data']['keepAlive'] ? 'true' : 'false');
        }
    }

    protected function startReactionTimer(): void
    {
        Co::run(function () {
            $timer = Timer::tick(TIMER_INTERVAL, fn () => $this->onReactionTick());
            Helper::addWsTimer($this->actionsTable, $timer);
        });
    }

    protected function onOpen(Server $server, Request $request): void
    {
        echo 'Connection open: ' . $request->fd . PHP_EOL;

        $timer = Timer::tick(TIMER_INTERVAL, fn() => $this->onMessageTick($server, $request));
        Helper::addWsTimer($this->actionsTable, $timer);

```

```
        // Let's send the current status to the client.
        $server->defer(function () use ($server, $request) {
            // send server status
            $server->push($request->fd, json_encode([
                'id' => $request->fd,
                'data' => [
                    'event' => 'server-status',
                    'data' => $this->actionsTable->get(HTTP_STATUS_TABLE_KEY,
'data') ?? SERVER_DEAD,
                ],
            ]));

            // send keep alive status
            $server->push($request->fd, json_encode([
                'id' => $request->fd,
                'data' => [
                    'event' => 'keep-alive',
                    'data' => Helper::getConfig($this->actionsTable, KEEP_ALIVE) ??
'false',
                ],
            ]));
        });
    }

    protected function onRequest(Request $request, Response $response): void
    {
        $templates = new Engine(ROOT_DIR . '/public');
        $response->end($templates->render('index', []));
    }

    protected function onMessage(Server $server, Frame $frame): void
    {
        echo 'Received message: ' . $frame->data . PHP_EOL;
        $this->actionsTable->set(WS_TABLE_KEY, [
            'data' => $frame->data,
        ]);
    }

    protected function onClose(Server $server, int $fd): void
    {
        echo 'Connection close: ' . $fd . PHP_EOL;
        Helper::clearWsTimers($this->actionsTable);
    }

    public function stop(): void
    {
        parent::stop();
```

```
        Helper::clearWsTimers($this->actionsTable);
    }
}
```

Listing 7.5: WebSocket Server Process.

Reference in the repo: https://phpa.me/jacked-php-chapter-7-WsServer

The code in Listing 7.5 shows a WebSocket server implemented inside an OpenSwoole Process. This server is part of our multi-process strategy designed to manage and control an HTTP server.

This WsServer will handle WebSocket connections, enabling real-time communication between the admin area (front-end) and the server processes. The WebSocket server uses several event handlers to manage connections and data:

1. **onOpen**: Triggered when a new WebSocket connection is opened.
2. **onRequest**: Handles HTTP requests to serve static files or the admin interface - this is the interface through which you manage the HTTP server.
3. **onMessage**: Processes incoming messages from WebSocket clients.
4. **onClose**: Triggered when a WebSocket connection is closed.

Notice that we have two ticks. Ticks are periodic tasks that run at specified intervals. They are callbacks that we register at the `OpenSwoole\Timer` component in the server's initialization. Used here to handle two primary responsibilities:

1. **onMessageTick**: This tick is responsible for informing the front end about the current status of the HTTP server.

- **Purpose**: Send real-time status updates to the connected WebSocket clients.
- **Mechanism**: It reads the current status from the `actionsTable` and broadcasts it to all WebSocket connections if there is a change.

```php
protected function onMessageTick(Server $server, Request $request): void
{
    $status = $this->actionsTable->get(HTTP_STATUS_TABLE_KEY, 'data');
    $currentState = $this->actionsTable->get(HTTP_TEMP_STATUS_TABLE_KEY, 'data');

    if ($currentState === $status) {
        return;
    }

    echo 'Sending status: ' . $status . PHP_EOL;
    $this->actionsTable->set(HTTP_TEMP_STATUS_TABLE_KEY, [
        'data' => $status,
    ]);

    foreach ($server->connections as $fd) {
        echo "Sending status to: $fd\n";
        if ($server->isEstablished($fd)) {
            $server->push($fd, json_encode([
                'id' => $fd,
                'data' => [
                    'event' => 'server-status',
                    'data' => $status,
                ],
            ]));
        }
    }
}
```

Listing 7.6: onMessageTick method present in the WebSocket Server Process.

2. **onReactionTick**: This tick handles actions received from the front end to control the HTTP server.

- **Purpose**: To process commands from the WebSocket clients, such as starting or stopping the HTTP server.
- **Mechanism**: It reads data from the `actionsTable` and performs corresponding actions like starting, stopping, or adjusting settings of the HTTP server.

```
protected function onReactionTick(): void
{
    $data = $this->actionsTable->get(WS_TABLE_KEY, 'data');
    $this->actionsTable->del(WS_TABLE_KEY);

    if (!$data) {
        return;
    }

    $parsedData = json_decode($data, true);
    if (!$parsedData) {
        return;
    }

    switch ($parsedData['event']) {
        case 'start':
            Helper::startHttpServer();
            break;
        case 'stop':
            Helper::stopHttpServer();
            break;
        case 'keep-alive':
            Helper::setConfig($this->actionsTable, KEEP_ALIVE, $parsedData['data']
['keepAlive'] ? 'true' : 'false');
    }
}
```

Listing 7.7: onReactionTick method present in the WebSocket Server Process.

As can be seen in the "message" event callback, all the incoming messages are considered an action to be processed by the Actions Process, registered at the ActionsTable.

Now that we have the realtime solution for the communication to flow, we need to start the HTTP Server and monitor it. The HTTP Server will be started by a Process, and we will monitor it by another Process. The monitoring process will check the HTTP Server status every second and update the ActionsTable with the current status. The communication process will be responsible for executing the actions based on the data in the ActionsTable.

The HTTP Server Process is shown at the Listing 7.8:

```php
<?php

namespace ServerManager;

use OpenSwoole\Table;
use OpenSwoole\Coroutine as Co;

class HttpServer extends ServiceProcess
{
    public function __construct(
        Table $actionsTable,
        protected string $host = '0.0.0.0',
        protected int $port = 8181,
    ) {
        parent::__construct($actionsTable);
    }

    public function callback(): void
    {
        Co::run(fn() => Helper::startHttpServer());
    }
}
```

Listing 7.8: HTTP Server Process.

Reference: https://phpa.me/jacked-php-chapter-7-HttpServer

The code in Listing 7.8 shows the HTTP Server process. This process is responsible for starting the HTTP server that we will manage. The HTTP server is started by executing the `startHttpServer` method from the `Helper` class. This method is responsible for starting the HTTP server and setting the process name to `HTTP_PROCESS_NAME`. The `HTTP_PROCESS_NAME` is a constant that defines the name of the process running the HTTP server. This name is used to identify the process when monitoring it, we use it to get its PID.

The following (Listing 7.9) is the Helper method that creates the HTTP Server:

```
public static function startHttpServer(): void
{
    $clean_pid = self::getHttpServerPid();
    if ($clean_pid === null) {
        System::exec('/usr/bin/php $(pwd)/server.php');
    }
}
```

Listing 7.9: Helper method to start the HTTP Server.

This strategy allows us to start the HTTP server only if it is not already running. The `getHttpServerPid` method is responsible for getting the PID of the HTTP server process. If the PID is not found, the server is started using the `System::exec` method. One question is if using the `OpenSwoole\Process` class to start the HTTP server we could accomplish the same. The answer is no, because the `OpenSwoole\Process` class starts as a fork of the parent process - it can't be instantiated from a coroutine. The `System::exec` method, on the other hand, executes a command in the shell, allowing us to start the HTTP server as a separate process. Consider as well that we chose to use `OpenSwoole\Table` to share data between processes, which require us to use `OpenSwoole\Timer::tick` to run the monitoring process. The tick method can only be used in a coroutine context, which is why we use `Co::run` to start the HTTP server - this limits us from using `OpenSwoole\Process` to start the HTTP server then.

Using the Processes

To start the processes, open your terminal and execute the `php service.php` command. This command initializes the WebSocket server, which also serves as the HTTP server for the admin area. This setup ensures that the WebSocket and HTTP servers run concurrently, allowing for efficient process management.

Service Initialization Code

The service.php script sets up and runs the necessary processes. The source code for this script is shown in Listing 7.10:

```
<?php

use Dotenv\Dotenv;
use ServerManager\Helper;
use ServerManager\Monitor;
use ServerManager\WsServer;
use ServerManager\HttpServer;

const ROOT_DIR = __DIR__;

include_once __DIR__ . '/vendor/autoload.php';

// Load config.
$dotenv = Dotenv::createImmutable(__DIR__);
$dotenv->load();

include_once __DIR__ . '/constants.php';

$actionsTable = Helper::startTable();

Helper::startConfig($actionsTable);

// Process 1: WebSocket server.
(new WsServer($actionsTable))->run();

// Process 2: HTTP server.
(new HttpServer($actionsTable))->run();

// Process 3: Monitor.
(new Monitor($actionsTable))->run();

Helper::listenKillSignal();
```

Listing 7.10: The service.php script initializes and runs multiple processes.

Accessing the Admin Area

To manage the HTTP server, open your web browser and navigate to `http://localhost:8080`. This admin interface allows you to start and stop the HTTP server conveniently. The HTTP server runs in the background; you can monitor its status through the admin page.

On the admin page, you'll find a user interface that provides controls for managing the HTTP server. The page displays the server's current status, allowing you to start or stop it as needed. The interface is designed to be simple and intuitive, ensuring you can easily manage the server.

Refer to Figure 7.2 below for a visual representation of the admin interface. This figure shows the layout and controls available on the web page, making it clear how to interact with the server management features.

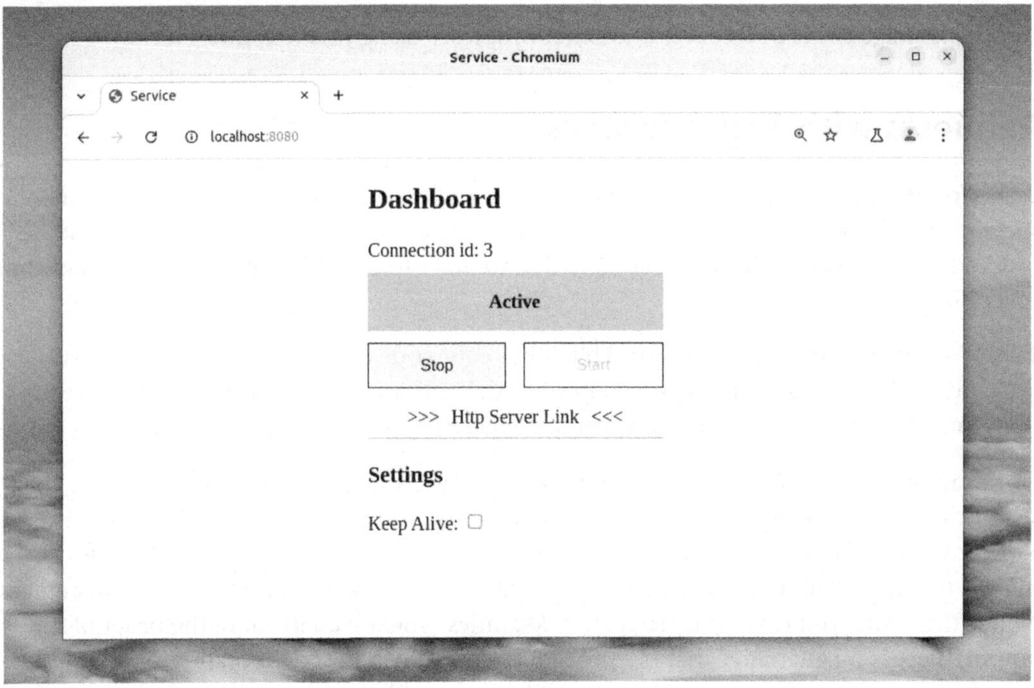

Figure 7.2: UI for the code sample where users can manage the HTTP Server on a simple web page.

The admin page is crucial for monitoring and controlling your server processes. It provides real-time feedback on the server's status and allows quick actions without needing to delve into the terminal each time. This streamlined interface enhances productivity by simplifying server management tasks. Key benefits include:

- **Real-Time Status Monitoring**: See at a glance whether the HTTP server is running or stopped.
- **Easy Control**: Start or stop the server with a single click, without using terminal commands.
- **User-Friendly Interface**: The layout is designed to be intuitive, making it accessible even for those who may not be comfortable with command-line operations.
- **Efficiency**: Quickly deploy changes and manage server states directly from your web browser.

You can manage the HTTP server and other processes using this web interface.

Requests with Task Workers

Task Workers are exactly what the name meant: parallel server workers responsible for specific tasks. From the server context, we can delegate tasks for them to execute while we proceed with the rest of the business logic that we have to do. This is not always possible but is very handy.

Task Worker Process is meant to avoid blocking your code execution with blocking I/O procedures. The case for it is when you need to delegate some tasks to alleviate the execution time of your server. Examples go from database procedures to external APIs executions.

Our example here brings the context of 2 servers, where one consumes data served by the second. Our main focus is on the first server. This first server is where the Task Worker is shown. Because external APIs can be time-consuming, when you need optimal performance, to have the option to execute multiple of them asynchronously has some advantages. Notice that when you run asynchronous tasks, unless you are controlling the order of the output, there is no guarantee that the procedures will finish in sequence, but for our case, this is not a problem, for some cases this might be a problem. An example of problems that might occur when executing asynchronous tasks is when the order of the results interfere in the result.

The first server, the one that consumes data from another, is shown at Listing 6.9, the server serving the data is shown at Listing 6.10.

```php
<?php

/**
 * This server consumes the data from the other server.
 *
 * This server process data requested asynchronously and present it.
 */

use OpenSwoole\Http\Server;
use OpenSwoole\Http\Request;
use OpenSwoole\Http\Response;

$server = new Server('0.0.0.0', 8080);

$server->set([
    'worker_num' => 1,
    'task_worker_num' => 2,
]);

$server->on('Request', function(Request $request,Response $response) use ($server) {
    $tasks[0] = ['filter' => 'name'];
    $tasks[1] = ['filter' => 'email'];

    $result = $server->taskCo($tasks, 1.5);

    $response->end('<pre>' . var_export($result, true) . '</pre>');
});

$server->on('Task', function (Server $server, int $task_id, int $worker_id, array $data) {
    $payload = file_get_contents('http://127.0.0.1:8181?filter=' . $data['filter']);

    $data['payload'] = $payload;
    $data['finished_at'] = time();
    $data['worker_id'] = $server->worker_id;

    return $data;
});

echo 'OpenSwoole http server is started at http://0.0.0.0:8080' . PHP_EOL;
$server->start();
```

Listing 7.11: Server executing procedures with Task Workers

Reference in the repo: https://phpa.me/jacked-php-chapter-7-example2-server

At this server, we simply delegate the task data to the Task and add some timeout (1.5 seconds) so we don't lose control over the execution. Each array inside variable `$tasks` will be considered a parallel input for the "Tasks" event callback. They will trigger execution in parallel workers (notice that we have two specified in the configuration at the top of the file). At the Task callback, we will request data from the second server and prepare the result with more information. That's all.

```php
<?php

/**
 * This server just serves data.
 *
 * This service returns or emails or names depending on the filter.
 */

use OpenSwoole\Http\Server;
use OpenSwoole\Http\Request;
use OpenSwoole\Http\Response;
use OpenSwoole\Coroutine as Co;

$server = new Server('0.0.0.0', 8181);

$server->on('Request',function(Request $request, Response $response) use ($server) {

    $input_data = $request->get;
    $accepted_filters = ['name', 'email'];

    if (
        empty($input_data)
        || !isset($input_data['filter'])
        || !in_array($input_data['filter'], $accepted_filters)
    ) {
        $response->header('Content-Type', 'application/json');
        $response->status(400);
        $response->end(json_encode([
            'success' => false,
            'message' => 'Missing or invalid required parameter: filter.',
        ]));
    }

    if ($input_data['filter'] === 'email') {
        $data = [
            [
                'email' => 'johngalt@wordstree.com',
            ],
            [
```

```
                    'email' => 'hariseldon@wordstree.com',
                ],
            ];
        } else {
            $data = [
                [
                    'name' => 'John Galt',
                ],
                [
                    'name' => 'Hari Seldon',
                ],
            ];
        }

        Co::sleep(1);

        $response->header('Content-Type', 'application/json');
        $response->end(json_encode($data));
});

echo 'OpenSwoole http server is started at http://0.0.0.0:8181' . PHP_EOL;
$server->start();
```

Listing 7.12: Server serving data for this example.

Reference in the repo: https://phpa.me/jacked-php-chapter-7-example2-server2

At this second server, we filter which chunk of the data we return and display an error if the input data is invalid.

After 1 second of sleep, the result of the request done to the first server (at Listing 6.9) is the following:

```
array (
  1 =>
  array (
    'filter' => 'email',
    'payload' => '[{"email":"johngalt@wordstree.com"},{"email":"hariseldon@
wordstree.com"}]',
    'finished_at' => 1635306232,
    'worker_id' => 2,
  ),
  0 =>
  array (
    'filter' => 'name',
```

```
    'payload' => '[{"name":"John Galt"},{"name":"Hari Seldon"}]',
    'finished_at' => 1635306232,
    'worker_id' => 1,
  ),
)
```

The order of the array elements above might change through a sequence of executions. It happens due to the nature of asynchronous calls.

The result of the request done to the second server (at Listing 6.10) is the following: (notice that this is the result of the filter "name")

```
[{"name":"John Galt"},{"name":"Hari Seldon"}]
```

Final Words

In this chapter, you learned how to manage Linux processes using OpenSwoole Process. You saw how to start and control processes, communicate between them, and share data using `OpenSwoole\Table`. You also saw how to use `OpenSwoole\Timer` to run periodic tasks and how to use `OpenSwoole\Coroutine` to run tasks in a coroutine context. You saw how to build a multi-process solution to manage and control an HTTP server in real-time. There is also an example of using Task Workers to execute tasks asynchronously and improve server performance.

Chapter 8

Other Resources

While writing this book, different resources played an important role. Community interactions, books, and articles all contributed significantly. Becoming fluent with technology is a lengthy journey, and written content is beneficial. However, more is needed to truly replace the value of community and collaboration with other developers. Don't get me wrong; it is vital to pursue written content, but ultimately, exchanging experiences with others is the essence of success.

Books

The most important source of information for this book was "Mastering Swoole PHP" by Bruce Dou, published in 2020 (https://swoolebook.com). This book offers technical explanations and delves deeply into the operational system context to elucidate some of the fundamental concepts behind Swoole's design decisions. It covers a substantial portion of Swoole and is an excellent reference for understanding Swoole.

Another significant resource was "Linux Socket Programming" by Warren W. Gay, published in 2000 (https://phpa.me/linux-socket-programming). This book provides crucial explanations of how Linux sockets work and how to program them, which were key to successfully understanding Swoole.

"The Linux Programming Interface" by Michael Kerrisk, published in 2010 (https://man7.org/tlpi/), was also indispensable. It explains many essential aspects of Linux, crucial for understanding processes, coroutines, and their programming interfaces.

Web Resources

The second most important source of information for OpenSwoole is the Documentation website (https://openswoole.com/). It is an excellent resource for information and reference. The website includes a forum where you can seek help and search for specific content, making it an indispensable bookmark for anyone working with OpenSwoole.

The third best reference is the OpenSwoole organization on GitHub (https://github.com/openswoole). Here, you'll find a wealth of valuable content. The source code is often the best source of knowledge, and if you're up for it, you'll find it here (https://github.com/openswoole/swoole-src). The code is written in C++; if you're not very familiar with C++, there are still other repositories that you can explore, such as the Swoole Library (https://github.com/openswoole/library), which contains many practical examples. The Official Docker Image of Swoole (https://github.com/openswoole/docker-swoole) is also an excellent source of information for dockerizing your environment. The repository with all the examples referenced in this book can be found here: https://github.com/Jacked-PHP/jacked-php-book-examples.

Community

Although I've saved this for last, the community is the most important resource for any programmer. The best way to stay in touch and keep up with the latest developments is through Slack and Discord. They also have a newsletter and a Twitter account (https://twitter.com/openswoole). You can find ways to get involved and stay connected with the community here: https://openswoole.com/community.

The collaborative spirit and shared knowledge within the community are priceless. Whether you're troubleshooting an issue, seeking advice, or sharing your experiences, the community provides support and insights you won't find in books or articles alone. Engaging with other developers can accelerate your learning and help you navigate the complexities of technology more effectively.

Made in the USA
Las Vegas, NV
05 May 2026

46461685R00109